# The Open Covenant

# The
# Open
# Covenant

---

## SOCIAL CHANGE IN
## CONTEMPORARY SOCIETY

Christopher Bates Doob

New York
Westport, Connecticut
London

Library of Congress Cataloging-in-Publication Data

Doob, Christopher Bates.
   The open convenant : social change in contemporary society /
Chrisopher Bates Doob.
      p. cm.
   Bibliography: p.
   Includes index.
   ISBN 0-275-92550-1 (alk. paper) ISBN
0-275-92661-3 (pbk. : alk. paper)
      1. United States—Social conditions.   2. Elite (Social sciences)—
United States.   3. Social movements—United States.   4. Social
change.   I. Title.
HN57.D66 1987
306'.0973—dc   19   87-19882
                        CIP

Library of Congress Catalog Card Number: 87-19882

ISBN:   0-275-92550-1
        0-275-92661-3 (pbk.)

First published in 1987

Praeger Publishers, One Madison Avenue, New York, NY 10010
A division of Greenwood Press, Inc.

Printed in the United States of America

The paper used in this book complies with the
Permanent Paper Standard issued by the National
Information Standards Organization (Z39.48-1984).

10  9  8  7  6  5  4  3  2  1

To Sam Vine, a good friend, whose insights have helped shape the central ideas in this book

# Contents

# Preface

Not long ago I had dinner with a close friend. We had not talked for some time, so I brought him up to date on this project. I explained that my central theme was the gradual but relentless breakdown of exclusionism in this country—the steadily increasing national tendency to show growing acceptance of others as well as a willingness to cooperate in new ways that might promote the likelihood of a more pleasant, more equitable, and safer life in the years ahead.

He listened glumly. "I know what you mean," he said when I finished, "but I'm not impressed by the depth of people's willingness to work cooperatively and help others. Look at the Live Aid business. There was a spurt of enthusiasm, but now, for most Americans, a concern for starving Africans barely has a place in the back of their minds."

I did not argue with him. I was not even tempted to. All I said was that when people are drowning, they are grateful for any pathetic piece of driftwood that floats by. They have no chance to consult consumer magazines on lifesaving equipment.

That was my immediate response. Later, however, the more I thought, the more it seemed I had understated my argument. Admittedly we twentieth-century types have not figured out the complexities of cooperation in the modern world, but we have made impressive strides. Traditionally the United States has been the bastion of capitalism, the champion of the individual and individual rights. With most of our institutions practicing exclusionism, community and cooperation have been low on the list of priorities or altogether absent. Gradually this is changing, however, and that is what this book considers.

From our Puritan past comes a central concept—the idea of the covenant. Covenants are solemn agreements between two or more people to do or not do something that is specified. Actually covenants can involve more than simply people. The Puritans believed that in the Scriptures God revealed two major covenants with humanity. However, our focus will involve covenants among human beings. In order to insure the success of what they considered their holy enterprise, Puritan settlers in different villages wrote covenants establishing codes for daily living. Without the covenants, they believed, their crucial experiment would fail. It was a question of urgency.

In the last couple of decades, there has been a steadily growing tolerance for other people and for a variety of different lifestyles, a mounting acceptance of the necessity to equalize women's and men's opportunities, and an increasing concern for environmental protection and the restriction or elimination of nuclear weaponry. These are movements toward an open covenant.

The open covenant signifies the establishment of broad alliances among people with different, often antagonistic outlooks and experiences. One might criticize the phrase. It does not refer to a literal covenant, although the supporters clearly, and often fervently, share common views. Furthermore, by definition the idea of an open covenant is a contradiction in terms. Covenants are restrictive rather than open, as those written by the Puritans certainly were. However, I have chosen the term open covenant to represent both the universality and the solemnity of this alliance. It is not a present reality, but perhaps some day it will be.

This book begins by considering the development and significance of ideologies in American society. In chapter 2 Puritan covenants are considered as ideologies. I examine the context in which they developed and the circumstances producing their failure, as well as the failure of the overall Puritan experiment. The Puritans tried to build a pure, religious community, excluding all who could not or would not live by their high standards. Eventually their exclusionist efforts failed.

Chapter 3 emphasizes that in spite of the demise of Puritan communities, the spirit of Puritan exclusionism has extended into the American economic and political systems, whose leaders sometimes provide a fatherly protection in exchange for the mandate to lead. Often these leaders demonstrate heroic qualities, and the theme of leaders as heroes is discussed at length here and also later in the book. Chapters 4–6 consider the influence of exclusionism in prominent American structures. Three topics are examined—the family, the education system, and bureaucracies.

Chapter 7 examines "the slow thaw," the gradual appreciation of others' rights exhibited in this country over the past four decades. Then, in chapter 8, I discuss three issues—the so called "second stage" of the modern women's movement, the environmental movement, and the antinuclear movement—illustrating how our society presently grapples with major problems that can only be resolved by transcending an exclusionist approach. Chapter 9 discusses the use of open covenants in the future.

I don't believe that any of us understand the social world very well. However, it is possible that if we study it calmly, carefully, and optimistically, we will learn increasingly more about its workings. We will see patterns that will help us to understand what has happened, what is happening, and what will happen in the future, and much of what we see will cause wonder and even awe, and will give us reason to look ahead with hope.

# Acknowledgments

A number of people have helped make this book possible. At Praeger, Alison Bricken has been an ideal editor, constantly providing clear, insightful direction. I am grateful for the fine work of Karen O'Brien, the project editor. Two colleagues in sociology, James Dingman and Bradford Powers, offered provocative observations and criticisms in their reviews. In addition, Nick Doob, L. Natalie Sandomirsky, and. Dorothy Trench-Bonett read the manuscript and made useful comments. Once again Teresa E. M. Carballal was the resident critic, reading, discussing, and evaluating the manuscript from soon after its inception until its departure for publication.

# The Open Covenant

# 1

## In the Eye of the Beholder

In Aldous Huxley's novel *Brave New World*, modern society was meticulously planned, with each caste of people developed in test tubes and then carefully conditioned so that the members would most effectively perform their particular duties.

One day the Director of Hatcheries and Conditioning was guiding some students through his facility. At one point the group entered a large, bare room, which was very bright and sunny. There were big bowls filled with flowers. The director ordered the nurses to place children's books, opened to brightly colored pictures of animals or birds, in between the bowls. Then he commanded that the children be brought in.

The nurses soon returned, each pushing a cart containing shelves of Delta children (a low caste) dressed identically in khaki. The infants were unloaded and turned so that they could see the flowers. When they saw the flowers, the children started crawling toward them, murmuring excitedly. Soon they were grasping the petals and crumpling the pages. The director waited until all the children were happily occupied, and then he said, "Watch carefully."

He gave a signal, and the head nurse at the other end of the room pressed a lever. There was a violent explosion followed by a siren and alarm bells. The children screamed, their faces distorted in terror. "And now," the director shouted (for the noise was deafening), "now we proceed to rub in the lesson with a mild electric shock."

Once again the director waved his hand, and the head nurse pushed a second lever. The children's screaming now changed to "sharp spasmodic yelps"; their little bodies jerked and stiffened with the shocks. The director watched dispassionately, and when he decided that the impact had been conveyed, he ordered the conditioning stopped. The explosions, sirens, and bells ceased, the twitching bodies relaxed, and the yelps became no more than sobs.

Had the lesson actually been learned? The director ordered the nurses to offer the children the flowers and books again. The nurses obeyed, and this time at the mere approach of the flowers and books the children drew away in horror and their howling increased.

Afterwards the director and the students discussed what they had observed. One of the students indicated that he could understand that it was reasonable to condition Deltas to hate books as they might read something that would decondition an important reflex, but why should they hate flowers? The director patiently explained that it was simply an economic issue. Previously Deltas and other lower caste groups had been conditioned to love natural things, and they would enthusiastically troop into the country, where they would have a fine time but would not spend any money. Clearly it made sound economic sense to condition the lower castes so that they would spend money on consumer products that would help keep the factories busy.[1]

It can be argued that the preceding discussion is actually about ideology, which is a system of beliefs that explains and justifies a group's outlooks and behavior. There has never been a society that has gone to the sophisticated genetic and conditioning extremes described above to put its ideology into practice. Nevertheless, it should be emphasized that the majority of people in many societies live severely controlled lives, where the punishments for opposing the dominant ideology are harsh. Even in the supposedly free society of the United States, many individuals encounter instant intolerance from those with different ideological positions. For instance, Americans often regard people who are sympathetic to socialism or communism with fear or suspicion.

In this chapter I discuss the development of ideological analysis, its role in American society, and its relevance to the basic ideas in this book.

## THE DEVELOPMENT OF IDEOLOGICAL ANALYSIS

Karl Mannheim, a German sociologist, indicated that only in recent centuries have people begun to observe the existence of ideologies. Such an appreciation develops when individuals become aware that adversaries' statements or actions are not lies or errors but instead are responses created by the social environment in which they are located. According to Mannheim, in the early sixteenth century when Machiavelli discussed the relationship between political leaders' opinions and their interests, he was initiating the use of the concept of ideology. In the following centuries, ideological analysis continued to be used in such works as David Hume's *History of England* and Georg Hegel's *Philosophy of Right*.

A major advance in the use of the concept was made by Karl Marx in the nineteenth century. Unlike his predecessors, who had emphasized that adversaries' ideological positions were either conscious or unconscious falsifications, Marx claimed that such positions developed because of prevailing social conditions. From the Marxist perspective, economic factors determine all social factors within a society, including ideology. Thus within capitalism those exclusive few who are wealthy and powerful will develop an ideology supporting and maintaining that system, while the majority, who are dispossessed workers, will produce an ideology which condemns and encourages the overthrow of an economic structure in which they are victimized.[2]

After Marx other scholars used the same general approach, often reaching conclusions that were very different from Marx's. Max Weber, for instance, disputed Marx's claim that economic systems have an overwhelming impact on all social systems. In *The Protestant Ethic and the Spirit of Capitalism*, which I discuss in chapter 3, he indicated that the development of capitalism has been strongly influenced by a religious ideology—Calvinism.

## IDEOLOGICAL ANALYSIS IN AMERICAN SOCIETY

Let us consider the American use of the concept of ideology in recent decades. In the 1950s Daniel Bell, a sociologist, wrote a book entitled *The End of Ideology*. The central thesis was that within Western democracies ideological positions about ways of improving society, particularly ways of making it more equitable for its members, have virtually disappeared because everyone, or nearly everyone, has been reaping the unprecedented benefits of affluent modern society.[3]

In a speech delivered in 1962, President John Kennedy concurred, stating that the resolution of America's most pressing problems should involve not "some grand warfare of rival ideologies which will sweep the country with passion but the practical management of a modern economy."[4]

Less than a decade after Kennedy's speech, Theodore Roszak concluded that the people who share such a perspective are members of the modern technocracy, who maintain a point of view that emphasizes that the only way to improve contemporary life is with rational, relentlessly modernized planning. According to Roszak, in recent decades the leaders of the technocracy have asserted three general claims:

1. Human beings' vital needs can be reduced to a set of technical questions which teams of specialists can translate into social and economic programs, management procedures, and mechanical devices. Spiritual and intellectual development are drastically restricted by such an approach.

2. The analysis of human needs has now been about 99 percent completed. When a social problem occurs within modern society, nothing more serious than a breakdown in communication has occurred, which requires only a minor repair. There is never any need

to make more extensive alterations in American institutions.

3. The specialists who both understand our needs and have the wisdom and skills to provide for them are located in two places—the upper levels of government and big business.[5]

Thus technocrats have dismissed the significance of ideology, reduced social problems to technical issues, and declared themselves the only qualified experts. In reality, however, weren't the technocrats actually asserting an ideological position with this set of self-serving claims? Without explicitly discussing ideology, the 1960s protest groups implied an affirmative answer when they directly opposed the technocratic position with their own fervent ideological outlook. The social world can not be reduced to a set of technical issues overseen by technically oriented specialists, they declared. The specialists have failed and continue to fail to consider some tremendously important human issues—in particular, black citizens' rights for equal opportunity and the brutal stupidity of continuing a hopelessly ineffective war in Southeast Asia.

In the past twenty years, both the trends just discussed have continued. The 1960s protesters, who tended to focus on only a few social problems, have been replaced by a diversity of organized interests—occupational groups, the elderly, gay people, ethnic groups, the three social movements discussed in chapter 8 (the women's movement, the environmental movement, and the antinuclear movement), and many more. Each group contains an ideology which describes its collective view of the social world, emphasizes that modern society fails to provide what the members seek, and claims that only by the members' concerted efforts can its cherished goal be accomplished.

However, while many groups and organizations have asserted new ideological positions in recent years, there has also been a distinct tendency to reduce social issues to technical analysis. With computers playing a central role, ours is now a postindustrial society, where the acquisition, storage, and transmission of information have become the keys to economic and political success. In the past fifteen years, many colleges and universities have developed an increasing number of business programs that are primarily technical, focusing on what students must learn to be economically successful in our computer-based information society. Such programs tend to ignore or downplay the importance of social and philosopical issues. The student is encouraged to be strictly practical: Pick a slot, prepare to perform the associated duties, and, assuming one gets a position for which one has prepared, go for it! Social activism tends to be discouraged.

I should add a couple of quick points. First, the preceding analysis sometimes proves to be oversimplified. Some people will pick their slot in the information society and, at the same time, will be deeply committed to the ideological position of an interest group. Such a combination, I suspect, is more the exception than the rule. Second, I am not implying that narrow, success-oriented goals and programs are new in recent years; they simply have become more prominent.

## SUMMARY

An ideology is a system of beliefs that explains and justifies a group's outlooks and behavior. Over the last few centuries, there has been an increasing awareness of the contribution that the analysis of ideologies can make to the study of society. One of the most significant contributions was made by Karl Marx, who emphasized that people's ideological positions are determined by immediate social conditions. Modern times have produced two tendencies about ideologies—an inclination, supported by the development of computers and an information-oriented society, to elevate the technocracy and downplay the significance of ideology; and a pattern of interest-group development, with each of the new groups maintaining its own ideology. In the next chapter, I will argue that an ideological position profoundly motivated the first European settlers in this country.

# 2

## The Politics of Perfection

Toward the end of the summer of 1636, about thirty middle-class English families took possession of about 200 miles of North American wilderness. Their hilly, rocky land reached from the southwestern boundary of what would be Boston to what later became the Rhode Island border. The area was devoid of human habitation except for scattered groups of Indians who were soon persuaded to leave their land for a small sum. The families founded a town, which they named Contentment. Later, more prosaic minds changed the name to Dedham.

For the original Puritan settlers, the venture was, to put it mildly, a new start. Kenneth Lockridge, a historian, wrote: "Since Adam awoke in Paradise there has been no moment in which mankind had been given a clean slate, but the founders of Dedham came as close as men had ever come."[1] This chapter discusses the Puritans' effort to implement their ideology as well as the failure of that effort.

### THE NOBLE EXPERIMENT

The Puritans' decision to come to the New World was based on their reading of the Bible, the book of Genesis in particular. According to the Bible, God had made a covenant with Adam, and this covenant guaranteed that all Adam's descendants would enjoy everlasting life as long as they obeyed God and, in particular, kept away from the tree of knowledge. Adam, of course, disobeyed God and ate the fruit of the tree of knowledge, and as a result humanity was cursed with toil, trouble, corruption, and finally eternal damnation.

However, in spite of Adam's disobedience, God in His mercy decided to provide a second covenant. While complete obedience from humanity now seemed impossible, God was willing to establish faith as the link to eventual salvation. Individuals chosen by the Almighty would be inspired to lead a life dedicated to the obedience of God's laws, and at the end of their earthly lives, these people would be destined for eternal salvation. In outward appearance and behavior, these people seemed no different from anyone else: What was different was their motivation. While others led virtuous lives because they feared earthly law or sought approval or rewards from others, God's chosen ones—the Puritans called them "visible saints"—lived virtuously because they were consumed by their faith in God. The second covenant, called the covenant of grace, was made between God and Abraham; according to the book of Genesis, it involved not only Abraham but also all his descendants.

The fortunate ones would be revealed by the way in which they lived. The Puritans considered themselves part of this select group. Seventeenth-century England, they believed, had become too corrupt for God's chosen ones. Their plan was to leave that downfallen country and start their holy experiment in a new, untarnished land.

A number of Puritan communities were formed. In the town of Dedham, the male heads of the thirty founding families established the Dedham Covenant, a document in which they set forth their ideology in detail and described the policies that they hoped would make the ideals become realities. The principal points were as follows:

1. The founders promised to bind themselves to the other members of the community by practicing Christian love in their daily lives. This was the fundamental position on which the town was founded.
2. Those who joined the community would be "of one

heart with us." In other words a systematic effort was made to exclude everyone who did not appear to be a humble seeker after a true faith in Jesus Christ, because, the Puritans believed, it was only out of such faith that true Christian love and community could develop.

3. Any differences that developed between citizens of the town had to be resolved by "a gentle mediation." While the founders were striving for social perfection, they were realistic enough to recognize that some of their members (those who they believed were unredeemed by God's grace) might attempt to inflict the malignance of their flawed characters on the entire community. Therefore measures had to be taken to protect the town.

4. Every man should pay his share to maintain the town and should accept the restrictions imposed on him and his family by this covenant and by all other statutes that local authorities enacted in the future. The founders of Dedham were emphasizing that once a policy was established, it was supposed to be embraced without reservation.[2]

In other Puritan towns, similar ideologies were enthusiastically recorded. The founders were committed to build wholesome and pure communities which would represent what they believed were God's ideals for community life. With this exalted standard, they were not reluctant to demand the full, uncompromising cooperation and participation of all members and to exclude from the town those who could not meet the standards.

The early settlers of Dedham found it relatively simple to determine the basic principles by which the town was to be run. It was more difficult, however, to establish guidelines for their church. The Puritans believed that the only source of information about a true church was the Bible, but when it came to fine points of theology that special book often proved obscure and even contradictory.

Eventually the founders of the town adopted a traditional Puritan position, deciding that membership in the church was to be restricted to "visible saints." The problem was to identify these visible saints. Like all Puritans the Dedham residents believed that only God knew who was destined for eventual salvation. However, the founders of the church reasoned, a person's public behavior and profession of faith—or "spiritual biography"—could serve to identify him or her as a visible saint.

After much deliberation among the citizens, they settled on eight men who were considered sufficiently saintly to serve as founders of the church. Then, amidst great celebration and with representatives from other churches in the colony present, the eight visible saints signed a covenant initiating the beginning of the Dedham church.

## THE EXPERIMENT'S FAILURE

The founders of Dedham made a valiant attempt to establish a community that would attain the Puritan ideals. Almost from the beginning, however, the purity of their standards was undermined. In the spirit of the Dedham Covenant, the original settlers had agreed to set aside six days each year so that the highways would be repaired; every male citizen was expected to work four of those six days. An early bylaw, however, permitted a man to hire a substitute.

By the 1650s the impact of accumulated wealth began to have a profound effect on the community. Rumblings were produced when a number of citizens sought larger shares of land. When these demands were not met, one of the petitioners, a Henry Phillips, rejected the authority of the Dedham board of selectmen and appealed to the General Court outside the town. Clearly the orderly society proclaimed in the Dedham Covenant was in peril.

Nevertheless, the town managed to maintain much of its purity of purpose until the 1670s and 1680s when the original political leaders died or left office. At that point ideals eroded rapidly. After 1675 the early bylaws restricting the presence of strangers in the town were seldom enforced. Mediators who were supposed to resolve individual disputes and thereby maintain placid, peaceful community relations were no longer used. Furthermore, for the first time, the local political leadership was now subjected to challenges, and dissent began to appear in the town records.[3]

Other Puritan communities also struggled to keep their purity of purpose, but it was a losing battle. The steady influx of outsiders who lacked the Puritans' strong religious ideology, and a younger generation with a weaker commitment to the parents' ideals were factors opposing the holy experiment. Perhaps the most crushing blow was the loss of the crown charter, which for half a century had provided the Puritans' formal control of government and also citizens' religious life in Massachusetts.[4]

The Puritan experiment failed, and yet, Lockridge contended, that experience brought to North America a European peasant tradition which emphasized that the best possible life that humanity can establish is one which is stable and centered in a small community. Lockridge wrote:

> In the depths of the American experience lies a craving for peace, unity, and order within the confines of a simple society. Though it is not à la mode to say so, next to it lies a willingness to exclude whatever men and to ignore whatever events threaten the fulfillment of that hunger.[5]

Certainly that willingness was apparent toward the end of the Puritan experiment. In 1692, in Salem, Massachusetts, a hysteria about witchcraft swept through the community. Before it was finished, twenty people had been hanged and two more had died in prison.

Why did the hysteria occur? No one knows with complete certainty, but it appears that the decline of Puritanism played a significant role. No longer were settlers able to have faith that their chosen way of life was the path to eternal glory. At the same time, the various economic endeavors that would establish prosperity in the colonies were not yet entrenched. Alone and frightened in the depths of the great western wilderness, the Puritans must have found it easy to spot witches in their midst.

The Puritans of Salem were frightened, and they responded with an exclusionism that was extreme even by Puritan standards: They killed those who frightened them. In the next chapter, I will show how our society has maintained some of the exclusionist tendencies of the Puritan tradition.

## SUMMARY

In 1629 the first Puritan settlers initiated what they considered an enormously exciting experiment. They were going to build a new, pure world, dedicated to the glory of God and spared from the corruption and wickedness that dominanted in Europe. In Dedham and elsewhere, they attempted to establish policies that would maintain the covenant of grace. However, eventually their pure, exclusionist ideology and way of life was submerged by the corrupting impact of wealth and also by the influx of outsiders who were indifferent to the Puritans' holy quest. The Puritans failed, but as I will show in the next chapter, they left a cultural legacy which still opposes efforts to establish an open covenant.

# 3

# Beyond the Lagoon

While doing research in the Trobriand Islands, Bronislaw Malinowski learned that when the local tribesmen went fishing in the nearby lagoon, they tended to be relaxed, relying on their skills and experience and seeking no help from supernatural forces. However, when they decided to brave the open sea with its uncertainty and danger, they practiced magic in order to master the elements of chance and luck.[1]

I suspect that we industrial and postindustrial Americans are little different from our preindustrial cousins. Frequently we pursue our daily routines with little sense of needing outside help, but sometimes life becomes unpredictable and frightening. We find ourselves "outside the lagoon," where we want help. What do we do? Some individuals will turn to therapists while others look to religion. There are times, however, when what frightens us individually also frightens large numbers of other people too. A collective response occurs, and at such times people often demonstrate a willingness or even an eagerness to turn to heroes for comfort, solace, and protection.

In this chapter I will examine the legacy of the Protestant Ethic, American values encouraging the development of heroes, and the characteristics of American presidential heroes.

## THE PROTESTANT ETHIC: AN AMERICAN
## LEGACY

The Puritans tried an exclusionist experiment in America, and eventually it failed. Nevertheless, the Puritan ideology had a profound impact on our society, as Max Weber indicated in *The Protestant Ethic and the Spirit of Capitalism*.

Weber analyzed the relationship between the Calvinist religion and the development of capitalism in America. According to Calvinist doctrine, the world exists for a single purpose—the glorification of God. This is a very tough and distant God, quite different from the approachable God of the New Testament. Weber wrote: "His place has been taken by a transcendental being, beyond the reach of human understanding, who with His quite incomprehensible decrees has decided the fate of every individual and regulated the tiniest details of the cosmos from eternity."[2]

This was not a God to fool around with. The individual could not con him or slip anything by him. There was really only one thing for people to determine—whether or not (in line with the covenant of grace discussed in the previous chapter) they were among the select few destined to enter heaven. The procedure was believed to be a fairly simple one. All the faithful Puritan family head needed to do was to assess his own worldly success. If he attained wealth, then he was assured that this was God's sign that he (and undoubtedly other family members too) was destined for everlasting glory in the next world. If he did not attain wealth, then God had gone thumbs down on him. In Calvinist doctrine the individual could not influence his own destiny, but at least he could discover it.

Looking back on Puritan times, we twentieth-century individuals are likely to conclude that it was a pretty grim era. While it is unreasonable to argue with that conclusion, I would point out that the Puritan ideology offered compensations. Believers were convinced that everything on earth was controlled by God—it was entirely His show. The task was to strive to be successful in one's endeavors, not for individual glory but for the glory of God. Thus there was no need to struggle over the meaning of life. Weber concluded that because they believed in God's complete control, the Puritans were spared "all the questions about the meaning of the world and of life, which have tortured others."[3]

By the end of the seventeenth century, the Puritan experiment had lost its original lustre. At that point few if any of the settlers believed that their new home was going to be a new, pure land, dedicated exclusively and unrelentingly to God's glory. While the Puritan experiment slid away into the past, the religiously induced spirit of capitalism lived on. No longer was capitalist effort dedicated to God's glory. Now instead of striving to demonstrate his worthiness of acceptance into heaven, the individual concentrated on earthly glory and success. According to Weber, the modern capitalist is different from the precapitalist merchant. The modern capitalist, who is not necessarily religious in an explicit sense, has retained the moral fervor of Calvinism—Weber's phrase was "an ethically colored maxim for the conduct of life"— while the precapitalist merchant, unmotivated by any religiously derived imperative, was simply stimulated by what Weber called "commercial daring," essentially the challenge of competition.[4] Weber believed, in short, that the Puritan ideology is still alive today in a nonreligious form.

Perhaps Weber's conclusion is oversimplified: Early capitalism might also have influenced the success of Calvinism. Most likely there was an interplay between the two. Actually the precise causal relationship is not important here. The significant point is that Calvinism and capitalism have been ideologically compatible, both encouraging the development of individuals, particularly men whose lives have been dedicated to the sanctity of work.

Capitalism has the same kind of compatibility with the doctrine of social Darwinism. As American capitalism took great, ruthless bounds through the nineteenth century, its proponents embraced a philosophy that justified their actions—the idea of "the survival of the fittest." Might is indeed right, this doctrine thundered, and the leading capitalists eagerly praised the perspective. John D. Rockefeller, for example, endorsed the approach in a Sunday school address:

The growth of a large business is merely a survival of the fittest.... The American Beauty rose can be produced in the splendor and fragrance which bring cheer to its beholder only by sacrificing the early buds which grow up around it. This is not an evil tendency in business. It is merely the working out of a law of nature and a law of God.[5]

It was a neat trick. Rockefeller was suggesting that the intimidation, violence, and even death inflicted by his hired toughs on striking workers and competing businesses was ethically the same as a Sunday afternoon's gardening. In both cases one's conscience remained untaxed, because that which was inferior was being pruned away for the supposed good of all. According to Rockefeller, as long as the capitalist increased his profits, he was inevitably bettering society.

## PROMINENT AMERICAN VALUES

With economic and political leaders supporting such positions, it is not surprising that the society at large has endorsed consistent values. In a list of fifteen value orientations in America, sociologist Robin Williams, Jr., has placed "achievement and success" at the top. In accord with the Calvinist tradition, our culture stresses personal achievement, particularly occupational achievement. Ours is the land of the Horatio Alger novels, where, according to those stories, dedicated, hardworking boys will inevitably obtain success. In many public opinion polls, Abraham Lincoln has been the American who most fully embodied the cardinal American virtues; he was thrifty, conscientious, eager for knowledge, ambitious, and managed to climb the ladder of opportunity from a poor birth in a log cabin to success as a merchant, lawyer, and eventually president.[6]

Achievement and success have been so important to Americans that they have often shown little concern about how they were obtained. Usually the end has justified the means. In spite of their title, the nineteenth-century robber barons have been more honored (as "shrewd, smart, and successful") than condemned for their frequently dubious practices.[7] Less than a decade ago, the trio of *Godfather* films was enormously successful at the box office. It seems that Americans are titillated by seeing a man so powerful and wealthy that he can confidently say "Let me make you an offer you can't refuse" rather than concerned about the morality of what he is doing and how he obtained a position which permitted him to make such a statement.

The second value orientation on Williams's list is "activity and work." Williams pointed out that a host of observers have noted that our country is the land of "hustle and bustle," of ceaseless activity. It is a country where the occupants are "interested in making things happen in the external world." They want "to dominate the world of nature, to subdue the physical world."[8] A vast majority of working Americans—80 percent at midcentury—would continue working even if they had the means to give it up. Enforced idleness is a debilitating condition for most Americans.[9] That outlook, certainly, is very consistent with our Calvinist tradition.

Also consistent are the gender-role ideals of young American men and women compared with their counterparts in European countries. Jeanne Block, a psychologist, asked samples of university students in six countries—Denmark, England, Finland, Norway, Sweden, and the United States—to describe their "idealized self" by choosing appropriate adjectives from a list she supplied. She found that compared to their counterparts in the five other countries, American males were more likely to pick the following adjectives: adventurous, self-confident, assertive, restless, ambitious, self-centered, shrewd, and competitive. All are adjectives that value individual over collective needs. American women follow the same pattern. In contrast to their European counterparts, the American female students were more inclined to choose the following adjectives as part of their ideal characterization: practical, adventurous, assertive, ambitious, self-centered, shrewd, and confident.

Block also found some interesting differences in the American students' perceptions of their parents' child-rearing values. The Americans were more likely than the Europeans to believe that they had been encouraged to achieve competitively and tended to more strongly emphasize differences in upbringing between girls and boys; furthermore the males were less inclined to feel that they were supposed to control aggression. Like the idealized self-images, these three patterns distinctly emphasize individual over collective needs.[10]

To summarize, it appears that the American people are unusually competitive, aggressive, achievement-oriented, and hard-working. In the early days of settlement, perhaps, those qualities were simply believed to be operating in the service of God. Now work is secularized; we glorify and enrich ourselves, not God. An important sense of belonging—to the Kingdom of God—is gone, or at least muted. The individual must struggle alone in cosmic solitude.

In addition, earthly communities have changed. The vast majority of Americans live either in urban or suburban areas. Since the advent of the industrial age, the interdependence of people living and working together in communities has been deteriorating. Now we have paid professionals in a host of public and private agencies who formally perform the jobs that neighbors and friends undertook cooperatively in the past.

Many Americans feel confused, lost, and isolated. When people feel this way, they are often ready to look for a comforting, kind, strong shoulder to lean on. Enter the all-American hero.

## A SPECIAL AMERICAN HERO

In *The Hero, American Style*, Marshall Fishwick described twelve prominent types of American heroes.[11] While some of the types involve people (primarily men) who are admirable in a variety of ways, none focus on what seem to be the qualities of a widely coveted American hero type: someone who is so strong, good, and brave that he can be seen as an ideal for all to emulate and follow. In the confusion and change of the late 1960s, however, Paul Simon recognized these qualities as heroic traits in his song "Mrs. Robinson":

Where have you gone, Joe DiMaggio,
A nation turns its lonely eyes to you.

Simon was suggesting that Americans needed a hero, and in several respects DiMaggio fit the bill. In 1941 Joe DiMaggio performed one of the most respected feats in baseball history: He produced a fifty-six–game hitting streak. In other words in fifty-six consecutive games he was able to get a base hit. To those who don't really understand the sport, that might not seem to be a particularly impressive feat, but its significance is borne out by the fact that in more than a century of major league baseball no other player has come close to that accomplishment.

The hitting streak and other achievements have established DiMaggio as one of the greatest players of all time, but he is known—in sports terminology "immortalized"—for more than his actual statistics. What has also been important is the way he accomplished things. As a player DiMaggio was the epitome of smoothness and grace. In the outfield he moved swiftly but effortlessly, running down fly balls with the grace of a Greek god. As a batter, his swing was the picture of smooth, coordinated perfection. In addition, there was DiMaggio's personal style. He was always the consummate gentleman, playing hard but fairly and maintaining his personal code of honor at all cost. During the fifty-six–game hitting streak, DiMaggio refused to bunt, believing that a hit obtained that way was beneath the dignity of the record he was establishing. He felt it was "a point of honor." Opposing infielders became aware of DiMaggio's refusal to bunt, and it seems almost certain that his streak would have continued longer if he had. Nonetheless, he refused: It was indeed a point of honor.[12]

I should make one more point about DiMaggio the hero. After retiring from the game, he has maintained only a limited contact with it. He has attended old-timers' games, relishing the ultimate honor of always being introduced last among the participants. He also spent two years as a batting coach for the Oakland Athletics, but that was not a successful venture. While DiMaggio's own batting mechanics were flawless, he lacked the capacity to effectively transmit his knowledge to others. In addition, while he was always pleasant and polite, he also was aloof.

What has been said about DiMaggio might well be true about heroes generally. While many of us want or even crave them, they are likely to lack the interest and skills to help us develop as individuals. However, that certainly does not stop many of us from seeking them out, particularly when they offer us the soft, protective shoulder.

This last point brings us to politics. Politically speaking, many Americans feel stranded "outside the lagoon." Kevin Phillips has suggested that America of the 1980s suffers from the same four basic conditions—an inflationary economy, skepticism about the political institution, deterioration of and confusion about values and standards, and frustration following the nation's first lost war—that dominated the Weimar Republic and permitted Hitler's rise to power.[13]

As Max Weber indicated, when times are tough and uncertain, people are likely to turn to charismatic leaders. The term "charisma," Weber emphasized, is a neutral term. Charismatic leaders aren't necessarily good individuals. They are simply people who appear on the scene at stressful times and draw others to them because their sense of mission offers direction and hope, even inspiration, to those who are frightened and lost.[14] Hitler had charismatic qualities and so does Ronald Reagan. Their individual personalities and goals are different, but, as Phillips emphasized, they both rose to the pinnacle of leadership in societies containing a common set of conditions.

It is worth examining Reagan because his situation offers some insight into the hero in modern American society. Reagan has been a hero to many Americans, who have seen him as the champion of the American way in its struggle against the Soviet Union—"the Evil Empire" as Reagan has called it in a burst of exclusionist rhetoric.

One might suggest, in fact, that Mr. Reagan has not only been an American hero but moreover a hero cast in a Puritan mold. In his campaign speeches, he has consistently emphasized "a nostalgic view of America, rooted in small-town values of hard work, patriotism, and neighborhoods."[15] Most modern politicans, according to pollster Patrick Caddell, are unable to convey a sense of conviction. Whether people have agreed with Reagan or not, they have felt that he transmitted a sense of conviction, and that ability seems to have been the primary basis of Reagan's appeal.

Reagan's acting experience has helped him convey this sense of conviction. His smooth, modulated voice is one factor, but more important perhaps have been his facial expressions. During the 1984 presidential campaign, researchers compared 174 students' reactions to video tapes of Reagan and the eight Democratic candidates. They found that Reagan's facial expressions were more likely to evoke reassuring feelings in the students and that they more frequently conveyed a sense of strength and happiness.[16] It is noteworthy that during that campaign, 82 percent of registered voters aged twenty-four and under supported Reagan.[17]

In 1984, 59 percent of the electorate supported for president a man who was packaged as a hero while only 41 percent voted for Walter Mondale, a man who distinctly lacked a heroic image and who shared his fellow Democratic challengers' inability to inspire confidence.

Ronald Reagan's heroic image, to be sure, was negatively affected by the revelation that members of his administration approved arms sales to the Iranian government, with which the United States had been on hostile terms for years, and then illegally diverted some of the funds received to the forces fighting the socialist government in Nicaragua. Following a televised address in March 1987 in which Mr. Reagan discussed the Iran arms sale, a national survey determined that twice as many people thought that the president was not revealing all he knew about the deal as the number of people who thought he was being completely candid. Then, in June 1987, a survey found that only 29 percent of the American public believed Reagan had been telling the truth about the affair,[18] indicating that even Ronald Reagan could ultimately tarnish an image that had once inspired widespread confidence.

Reagan is only the most recent president to project a successful heroic image. Going through the presidents of the past half-century, we see that those who received the most popular support were those widely regarded as heroes. These men were liked and admired, managed to project a protective "daddy" image, and, above all, inevitably appeared effective at critical times, often asserting their leadership in very patriotic terms.

*Franklin Roosevelt.* Roosevelt entered office during a major crisis, the Great Depression. With his famous "fireside chats" delivered by radio, he used a powerful, warm voice and simple, catchy phrases to convince millions of Americans that he understood their confusion and suffering and that his New Deal would produce the programs that would eventually put the country back on its feet. Although the New Deal had mixed success, Roosevelt received strong popular support (winning forty-six of forty-eight states in 1936) and died in 1945 during an unprecedented fourth term in office.

*Harry Truman.* Unimpressive in appearance and bearing, he entered office inauspiciously as the sudden successor to Roosevelt. Many have believed he grew in office. He was tough and plainspoken, and proved willing to take full responsibility for decisions—he was known for the phrase "The buck stops here"—such as the two atom bombs dropped in Japan and the American entrance into the Korean War. In particular, he enjoyed combatting the Soviets, happily describing his first sharp exchange with Soviet Foreign Minister Molotov in this way: "I gave it to him straight 'one-two to the jaw.' "[19] To the surprise of many, he was elected to a second term, and his popularity increased further during the 1970s and 1980s as the heroic image of the strong, tough, and fair leader has blossomed in books, magazine articles, a movie, and even a rock song.

*Dwight Eisenhower.* Eisenhower was a war hero who had conducted himself diplomatically as a general, and he used a similar style as president. Eisenhower left tough, partisan speeches to others, such as his secretary of state or vice-president. His speeches were filled with broad, bland statements that gave most Americans a reasssurance of a stable, prosperous world. Eisenhower had no difficulty in his two election campaigns, twice decisively defeating a bright, articulate, but decidedly unheroic "egg head" (intellectual)—Adlai Stevenson.

*John Kennedy.* Like Truman, Kennedy's heroic image has grown since his death. Assassination can do that, often obscuring in the public mind significant events in a person's life. To be sure, Kennedy projected a heroic image—a glittering war record, a highly successful political career, a wealthy, distinguished, and attractive family, a dashing personal appearance and style, and a successful confrontation with the Soviets in the Cuban missile crisis. He had distinct drawbacks as a president, but it seems almost inevitable that had he lived, he would have been reelected in 1964.

We have now considered presidents who held office between 1932 and 1963. What about the seventeen years preceding Reagan's election? In my estimation the men elected to our highest office were not heroes in the sense that I have been using the term. None was particularly liked and admired, and certainly they failed to provide a sense of reassuring, protective leadership at crisis times. Why, then, were Lyndon Johnson, Richard Nixon, and Jimmy Carter elected? Quite simply, it may have been because their opponents were even less palatable to the American people. In 1964, with the country in a liberal mood, Johnson, an accomplished moderate, soundly defeated the dour conservative Barry Goldwater by 17 million votes. In 1968, after the assassination of Robert Kennedy (a distinctly heroic type) Richard Nixon found himself opposing friendly, talkative Hubert Humphrey, a moderate Democrat whose position on the important issue of continuing American involvement in the Vietnam War lacked decisiveness. Nixon barely defeated Humphrey. Then in 1972, after his inner circle played "dirty tricks" on Edmund Muskie (who might have proved a formidable opponent) he soundly defeated George McGovern, a leftist version of Barry Goldwater. Finally, in 1976, the intense, cautious, devout, honest, but decidedly unheroic Jimmy Carter defeated Gerald Ford, whose inability to inspire public confidence was in large part the result of running for the presidency as a Republican in the aftermath of the Watergate scandals.

As of 1987, three of the last four, and four of the past seven presidents have been Republicans. However, their election to the top office probably occurred in spite of the fact that they were Republicans. At other levels of government, the Democrats generally have been dominant across the nation. What is remarkable about the individuals elected president is that, whether Republicans or Democrats, many of them have been heroic types, and those who have not been won the office because the opposition was even less successful in meeting the heroic standard. Furthermore if one goes back through the above list, it becomes apparent that many of these men had their finest hours in the public mind when they were emphasizing exclusionism—leading the country into war or, in Reagan's case, expressing a highly critical, even belligerent attitude toward our nation's most formidable potential military opponent, the Soviet Union.

Survey data support the conclusion that leading politicians are perceived as heroic. At the end of 1984, a national sample of Americans was asked to identify the two individuals of each sex they most admired. Totals combining each respondent's scores placed politicians in seven of the top ten slots for men and allotted seven of the top ten positions for women to politicians or politicians' wives. The top scores went to Ronald Reagan and Margaret Thatcher, both conservatives who have fervently emphasized the necessity of restoring prosperity, stability, and honor to their respective countries and who have continuously lauded patriotism, an important type of exclusionism.[20]

People do indeed honor those who can convince them they possess ability to lead them back inside the lagoon. A recognized American hero can convince people of his or her capacity to lead them back to protection, safety, and happiness. The accomplishments, however, usually fall far short of the claims; were the claims valid, there would have been no reason to write this book.

## SUMMARY

Max Weber concluded that Puritan ideology still influences modern Americans. Instead of seeking eternal glory, they seek worldly acclaim—the pursuit of wealth and power. Both the doctrine of social Darwinism and prominent American values demonstrate consistency with Puritan ideology, but the endorsement of such values and the associated lifestyle can produce a feeling of confusion and isolation. People turn to others for comfort and protection. The hero emerges, and in 1980 we received Ronald Reagan. He hasn't been the first president to offer a comforting, reassuring shoulder to lean on. A half-century ago it was Franklin Roosevelt, and later Harry Truman, Dwight Eisenhower, and John Kennedy. No modern politician has more successfully courted public support than Reagan, however. With his small-town values and his condemnation of the Soviet's "evil empire," he has had the Puritans' zest for exclusionism. Reagan seems to claim that the covenant of grace embraces all Americans but condemns the Soviets to eternal damnation.

In the next chapter, my focus will shift from examining exclusionism in the public arena to analyzing the concept in a private sphere—the family.

# 4

## The Extended Womb

During the first ten months of life, children in eastern Holland are held only when they are being fed or changed. The rest of the time they are tightly bound in bassinets, which are placed in isolated rooms away from the more active parts of the house. These children have no toys and minimal stimulation, and the amount of contact with adults is considerably less than in our society. Do such children grow up to be idiots? They decidedly do not. In fact, surprising though it might seem, at the age of five their behavior is very much like that of American children.[1]

However, if these Dutch children had been brought up in the Dutch manner in American society, they might indeed have had serious problems. To some extent societies are like puzzles; their parts fit together. Thus the socialization pattern of eastern Holland prepares children to grow up in eastern Holland and not the United States. American socialization is equally specialized.

This is the first of three chapters that examine American institutions. We will see a compatibility between the American family and the general American society. In both cases an ideology emphasizing exclusionism has been a dominant theme, but now because of exclusionism the American family is in crisis. In fact, one might argue that attacks against exclusionism are currently stronger here than in any other institution. In this chapter I examine exclusionism in American families and opposition to that exclusionism.

## TRADITIONAL AMERICAN FAMILIES: FITTING EXCLUSIONISM

From the time of the earliest American settlements, the nuclear family, as opposed to the extended family, has been the dominant structure. William Goode has suggested that the specific demands of an industrial setting have tended to encourage this more streamlined family type.[2]

Physical mobility has been one characteristic of industrial societies supporting the nuclear family. In an industrial society, where there are frequent incentives to change jobs, it is much easier and quicker to move the smaller nuclear unit than an entire extended family. Upward mobility, strongly emphasized in industrial societies, has also supported the development of the nuclear family, which is small and flexible and which permits people to change their speech, dress, and lifestyle without extensive resistance or criticism from socially conservative kin. Such changes often help individuals to get a job (or improve their job) in an industrial context, thereby contributing to their advancement. In addition, for an individual to perform effectively in an industrial setting, traditional obligations to a variety of extended family kin need to be severely limited, and indeed the nuclear family radically restricts such obligations.

In the nineteenth and early twentieth centuries, political, economic, and educational leaders believed that to insure prosperity in industrial society the nuclear family was necessary. Someone had to be anchored at home to run the household and to fulfill all family members' needs. Obviously the husband couldn't do it; he was out earning a living. By default, then, that role fell to the wife and mother.

The challenge was to keep women locked into that role. That wasn't too difficult in the mid-nineteenth century, because women realized that it was almost inconceivable that they could enter the work world in anything but menial positions. By 1900, however, times were changing. Many women, especially educated women attracted by that era's feminist movement, were caught in the tide of expanding expectations. Consequently the experts of that time needed to change their ideological emphasis. They contended that women, like men, had the right to expect self-fulfillment but self-fulfillment of another kind. Their "careers" would be centered in the home, and in preparation they would receive special training in "homemaking," "domestic science," and "home economics."[3] For many years the ruse was quite effective. As recently as 1963, Betty Friedan's famous *Feminine Mystique* discussed the letdown that she and her college classmates felt when they discovered that as housewives they didn't find the stimulation and excitement that family experts in the mass media and classroom had promised them.[4]

While the traditional housewife was not thrilled with her daily life, her husband was considerably more fortunate. He was the breadwinner, a kind of local hero. Much like the victorious general returning from war, his daily return from winning the family bread would usually be announced, not by literal trumpets to be sure but with the same effect. "Daddy's home!" the mother or one of the children would shout. One of the "minions" would get the husband's pipe and slippers—or in the case of television show *All in the Family*'s Archie Bunker, a beer—and from his grand entrance until his departure the next morning, he could expect everyone, especially his wife, to wait on him. The husband could also expect to dominate dinner conversation with stories about what happened to him, no matter how boring the accounts were. After all, he was the breadwinner.

## MEMBERS STRIKE BACK: OPPOSING FAMILY EXCLUSIONISM

Basically the husband had a good position in the traditional American nuclear family. Overall, however, the structure has been riddled with problems. Richard Sennett wrote about middle-class Chicago families from 1872 to 1890. Using census data, Sennett was able to discover that the sons of nuclear families were less successful economically than the sons of extended families. Drawing for explanation on historical writings and novels, Sennett concluded that in nuclear families the lone breadwinners tended to sequester themselves, to seek protection and isolation from the cold and often savage industrial world. When these men came home from work, discussion of work and work-related subjects was negligible. With their fathers as models, sons in nuclear families grew up reluctant to brave the struggles and challenges of the outside world, and occupational success was likely to be fairly modest.

It was quite a different picture, Sennett suggested, in extended families. The household did not contain a solitary man but two, three, or maybe more. Dinner-table conversation often focused on what happened at work. The outside world was not pushed out of family affairs but rather was very much present. Consequently young men growing up had a much more detailed sense of how the occupational world worked than their counterparts maturing in nuclear families. When these young men entered the work force, they were less afraid and better equipped emotionally and intellectually to succeed. Not surprisingly they were much more successful.[5]

Apparently the extended family, or at least portions of it, served an important function, providing young men the information they needed to adjust to the rapidly expanding industrial world. In the modern era, this function has generally been performed by peer groups, particularly when the family lacks the values and experience to prepare its members to participate effectively in contemporary life.

In the 1960s parents in nuclear families might have been particularly deficient in this regard, because their experiences were so different from their children's. The youth of that time were the first generation to grow up with the threat of nuclear war, the availability of the contraceptive pill (which eliminated concern with contraception almost completely), the growing fear of environmental pollution, and a steady dose of media (especially television) suggesting great material abundance.[6]

Consequently the decade of the 1960s was a difficult time to convince children to accept parental values, and yet, often without an awareness of the barriers they faced, many middle-class parents were determined to impose their exclusionist values and lifestyle on their children.

Sociologist Philip Slater believed that the sixties film *The Graduate* effectively represented the relationship between many parents and children during that era. At one point in the film, the hero rushes to a church to rescue his beloved who is being forced to marry another man. He arrives just in time. The valiant young man grabs a cross, beats off the crowd, and then uses the cross to bar the door from the outside, permitting the couple to escape. The woman's parents, in fact that entire generation of parents, were being presented as vampires. As all moviegoers know, a cross will ward off vampires and, placed on a door, will prevent them from passing through. Slater suggested that among upper-middle-class American students, from whom the most active participants in the sixties protests were drawn, the parents often

> feed on the child's accomplishments, sucking sustenance for their pale lives from vicarious enjoyment of his or her own development. In a sense this sucking is appropriate since the parents give so much—lavish so much care, love, thoughtfulness, and self-sacrifice on their blood bank. But this is little comfort for the child, who at some point must rise above his guilt and live his own life—the culture demands it of him.[7]

If Slater's analysis is correct, then these young people were facing a strain similar to that endured by the nineteenth-century Chicagoans described by Sennett. In both cases the nuclear family's envelopment impeded the child, making it difficult for him or her to seek or achieve personally meaningful success.

Nuclear families have been a source of pain and frustration for adults too, as the rising divorce rate indicates. Over the past seventy-five years, the divorce rate has risen steadily—from 1 divorce for every 11.5 marriages in 1910 to nearly 1 divorce for every 2 marriages in 1984.[8]

What has been going wrong? Phillipe Ariès, a French historian, offered an answer. The modern family, he contended, has become a "prison of love." In preindustrial times women and children were respected contributors to family production. With industrialization, women's production role was diminished, and they were expected to stay home and care for the children. The nuclear family was no longer a production unit but had become strictly an agent of socialization, where mother and father were centered around children, concentrating on their development and demanding, in turn, their affection. It was expected that all family members would love each other, and the pressure to achieve this condition became so intense that divorce, which in preindustrial times was only sought under extraordinary circumstances, became a necessary safety valve to release people from what often proved an unattainable expectation. According to Ariès, a strong motivation for the modern women's movement has been the drive to free women from domestic bondage, where they have been languishing since the advent of the industrial age. Ariès suggested that in the future, nuclear family structures might become temporary, forming only for approximately fifteen-year periods to produce and raise children and then dissolving when their express purpose has been met.[9]

Is there any evidence that Ariès's option is gaining support? Although not exactly in the form he suggested, there is evidence indicating that some Americans are seeking to develop new types of marriages that will more effectively meets their needs than has the traditional variety. Following a large study of American couples, sociologists Philip Blumstein and Pepper Schwartz concluded that their data suggest that voluntary marriage (which will last only as long as the couple is in love), cohabitation as a form of trial marriage, and same-sex marriage are options that might become increasingly popular in the future.[10]

There is also evidence that an increasing proportion of young people might remain single. In 1970, 45 percent of men and 64 percent of women in their early twenties had already married. In 1980, however, only 31 percent of men and 50 percent of women in that age group had married. It may be that young people are simply deciding to marry later, but according to Paul Glick, a well-known demographer, it is also probable that a distinctly greater percentage of young people than in the past are committing themselves to staying single or cohabiting. Glick projected that for young people 25 to 29 years old, the percentage of unmarried individuals will be three times as large as in their parents' generation.[11]

What are the actual attractions of remaining single? Peter Stein introduced a study of singlehood with this quotation from a thirty-one-year-old female college instructor:

> Well, today I think I'll stay single forever. It's a hell of a lot more freedom than it would be either in a marriage or an exclusive relationship.... This affords the opportunity of getting to know well and be friends with a lot of different people. No restrictions except the restrictions that I happen to choose.[12]

Stein found that the single people he interviewed were fixated on exclusionist tendencies in modern couple relationships. The informants identified "pushes away" from marriage such as the restriction of growth and development, limitation of friendships to individuals mutually satisfying to both partners, and the restriction of experience and opportunities. "Pulls toward" singlehood included economic self-sufficiency, psychological autonomy (especially for women), and the availability of sexual variety.

## A CONCLUDING COMMENT

For at least twenty years, it has been clear that the family resides in crisis. Its womb-like quality, which means that it can be a source of comfort and protection, can also make it a prison. People are not reluctant to strike out against family exclusionism and try to make their lives better, but often they are very unclear about what they want. Is it something simple like peace and quiet, or is it perhaps an elusive Hollywood image? A friend who had been advising a younger relative recently told me: "I kept asking him what he wanted, and he couldn't tell me.... He just kept saying over and over that he's unhappy."

Then what lies ahead? It probably would not amaze readers to learn that I really don't know; however, I'm not reluctant to make a guess. The nuclear family, I suspect, will persist. Certainly it will not prove ideal for everyone, and in the decades ahead, Americans will become increasingly tolerant toward those who choose to forsake it. At the same time, most Americans will continue to marry and raise children in families.

Personally I would not want it any other way. If large numbers of Americans decide to remain single all their lives or for much of them, they will certainly be free to pursue personal interests. In my opinion, however, they will be abandoning a prime context for nurturing an important skill of modern life: the ability to blend one's personal needs and priorities with those of others. If an open convenant is going to develop in the years ahead, the family must be the prime "breeding ground" for developing the negotiating and compromising skills that will make it possible. Thus a major challenge in the family realm, it seems to me, is to forsake closed, often confused traditional convenants and establish new, more open covenants, which will be uplifting to family members and provide momentum for making a positive contribution to the social world.

## SUMMARY

Like other industrial societies, ours has favored the nuclear family, where an exclusionist ideology has emphasized that the woman should be locked into the domestic role and the man should be the breadwinner and hero. For many Americans, however, such a family has presented serious problems as indicated by Richard Sennett's observations of nineteenth century middle-class families, Philip Slater's commentary on the protesters of the 1960s, Phillipe Ariès's conclusions about the nuclear family as a "prison of love," and Peter Stein's analysis of singlehood. As a result, young people today appear somewhat more disposed to seek nontraditional options or avoid marriage than in the past. Nonetheless, marriage will probably remain popular in the decades ahead.

# 5

## Hire Education

Early leaders of the public education movement—people like Horace Mann—supported exclusionism, establishing a covenant with political and economic leaders. Mann and his cohorts assured leaders that if they supported the development of public education, educators would do everything in their power to make certain that children would neither rebel against capitalism nor endorse another economic system.

In this chapter I will examine the ideology of educational exclusionism, consider reform efforts, and then assess the current plight of modern education.

### THE COVENANT IN PUBLIC EDUCATION

In his 1848 report as secretary of the Massachusetts public-school system, Horace Mann argued that education would prevent the masses from resorting to violence. Then in 1877 U.S. Education Commissioner John Eaton wrote that schools should train children to oppose the evils of labor strikes and other violence. Capitalists, he suggested, needed to "weigh the cost of the mob and the tramp against the expense of universal and sufficient education."[1]

The leaders of American public education convinced teachers that they had a sacred mission to preserve the capitalist system, and the teachers, in turn, sought to convince the students likewise. For instance, mid–nineteenth-century teachers reading the very popular *American Journal of Education* encountered this catechism that presented an ideological position strongly supporting capitalism:

> Q: Suppose a capitalist, in employing his capital, makes large profits, would that harm the working man?
>
> A: No. There would be more capital to pay wages.
>
> Q: Are you sorry, then, that capitalists should have great profits?
>
> A: Glad....
>
> Q: If there are two boys starting in life, one the son of a man who has accumulated capital, the other of a man who has not, shall I be right in saying that the boy without this advantage can never be a capitalist?
>
> A: No.
>
> Q: But what is to make him a capitalist?
>
> A: Saving.[2]

The implied ideological message was "Hang in there, kid. Anyone can make it as long as he plugs away, believes in the system, and, in addition, leads a good, clean life." The early public schools sermonized endlessly about the need for a clean, virtuous life. Even the arithmetic problems incorporated points about morality. An example from one book read: "There were 7 farmers, 3 of whom drank rum and whisky and became miserable. The rest drank water and were healthy and happy. How many drank water?"[3]

Why did educators place such emphasis on the virtues of capitalism and the importance of clean living? The answer lay in the conditions of workers' lives in the nineteenth century. The average factory worker had a miserable existence, laboring twelve to fourteen hours a day for minimal pay under abysmal conditions. Understandably capitalists feared riots and even revolution. Quite possibly the schools' emphasis on faith in the economic system helped stave off such outbreaks. It seems very likely that the capitalists got their money's worth when they supported public education.

In the nineteenth century, control over students was crudely maintained, with corporal punishment often administered. In modern times educators have found that control over students can be much more elegantly imposed. There is the "hidden curriculum," a set of school rules that is seldom made explicit but is recognized as important by students. Pupils have traditionally been expected to sit only in assigned seats, to answer questions when called on to do so, to take tests when told to take them, and to keep quiet the rest of the time. Many American teachers emphasize a covert set of three r's— "repetition, redundancy, and ritualistic action above all else."[4]

Exposure to the hidden curriculum begins in kindergarten, where children are expected to take part in a number of carefully supervised activities. Those who submit to the imposed discipline and eventually learn the habit of unthinking obedience tend to be evaluated by the school as good students. Those who accept the routines of the school but do not personally identify with them will probably find themselves placed in the category of adequate students. Finally children who refuse to accept the rules of the school will often receive the label "problem children" or "bad students." In modern times schools frequently engage clinical psychologists or other therapists to help teachers deal with such children.[5]

In school, children are expected to learn to behave in a manner that will make them proper young citizens. In the course of this training, they are sorted out by a variety of tests—academic, psychological, physical, and social. Those who pass the most significant tests will have a chance to move ahead in school—to college, perhaps to graduate school, and to the best-paying, most prestigious positions.

Many critics claim that since steady performance at a variety of dull jobs requires the downplay of people's creative, innovative side, schools have taken it on themselves to kill the creative spirit. This seems to be the modern version of Horace Mann's covenant. Charles Reich wrote:

No person with a strongly developed aesthetic sense, a love of nature, a passion for music, a desire for reflection, or a strongly marked independence could possibly be happy or contented in a factory or white-collar job. Hence these characteristics must be snuffed out in school. Taste must be lowered and vulgarized, internal reflection must be minimized, feeling for beauty cut off. All of these processes are begun in school, and then carried into life.[6]

Certainly this is a very strong statement, yet it is not hard to find research that supports the position. In one study 449 high-school students were given an IQ test and a series of exams designed to measure creativity. Then, in a later test, the top 20 percent in each of these two categories was asked to assess the personality traits teachers prefer in students and the traits they themselves favored. Interestingly the two groups virtually agreed about the traits that teachers would most value. However, the two groups disagreed substantially on the traits they preferred. Most strikingly the group that tested high in intelligence tended to favor the same traits as the teachers. The highly creative students, on the other hand, preferred traits that the teachers ranked low. Clearly, compared to the teachers and the high-IQ students, they were nonconformists, rejecting the exclusionist ideology maintained by the educational system.[7]

While I like to think that there are a fair number of teachers and administrators at all educational levels who struggle to maintain schools where children's creative thought and action are nurtured, it is not hard to bring to mind a slew of educators who are champions of educational law and order—the hidden curriculum.

The teacher as drill sergeant is what I am discussing. The situation is essentially the same in elementary or graduate school. In both cases the teacher as an aloof hero sets the standards and provides information. The students listen and learn, and as they get older, they write down what they believe the teacher thinks are the essentials and then later repeat it. "Regurgitate" is the rather vivid verb that has been widely used.

Sometimes the teacher–drill sergeant can even become

teacher–drill sergeant–hero. In high school I had an ex-Marine as a German teacher. He was a drill sergeant who took us on grammatical maneuvers each class. When the linguistic terrain started getting rough, he would turn to us with a weather-beaten smile and say, "Now here's where we separate the men from the boys." I would take a deep breath and plunge ahead with gusto toward the jungle of irregular verbs or strings of adjectives in the dative case. I would approach each day's maneuvers eagerly. With this teacher leading, I would have followed anywhere. He was a tough and genuine hero for me, and he seemed to have mastered a way of teaching grammar that was effective for at least some students. The drill-sergeant technique, however, did not work very well when we studied literature. The problem with drill-sergeant teaching is that the technique has no capacity to deal with nuance, and literature, of course, is packed with it. Authoritarian teachers are effective only when they are repositories of completely unchallengable answers.

## A CASE OF EDUCATIONAL REFORM

In the sixties and early seventies, concern with authoritarianism in teaching received increased attention. James Herndon was one of many teachers who tried his best to combat this type of exclusionism in education. Herndon was a junior-high-school teacher in California. One fall he and and Frank, a colleague, initiated a two-hour elective class for eighth graders. The course was entitled Creative Arts, and it was planned as a course without grades or assignments, thus permitting the students to do whatever they wanted to do. The teachers were excited about the course, because they had had considerable success with innovative projects in their regular classes. For instance, in one previous class the students wrote to the Peace Corps and received information about the problems of various countries and what the workers hoped to accomplish there. Then the students kept written diaries about their imaginary activities as Peace Corps volunteers. In another class the students were asked to invent their own language, making lists of common words and then developing symbols to stand for each word. After that the class compiled a list of the best symbols and translated a number of fairy tales into the new language.

Herndon concluded that he and Frank were creative teachers and thus should have no problem with their two-hour elective. He was wrong. For most of the year both felt it was the worst class they had ever taught. A major problem was that they had decided to take a step against what they considered the most repressive measure maintained in all classes—the requirement that every time a student left the room he or she needed a hall pass. Casually, at the beginning of the course, the teachers issued permanent hall passes. As far as the teachers were concerned, it wasn't a big deal, but it was for most of the students. They couldn't believe their luck and spent most of the first class interrogating Herndon about the exact meaning of the permanent hall pass. When, to his exhausted relief, they'd gotten the message that they could use the passes any time they wanted, most of them gleefully took off into the halls. They would eventually reappear but would soon disappear again, immensely enjoying their new-found freedom.

At first the teachers were stumped. The course had seemed so promising in the beginning. What had gone wrong? Eventually they figured it out. In the regular courses, the students were happy enough to do the creative work because it was more interesting than traditional assignments, but when they were given the chance to do whatever they wanted, it was an entirely new ball game.

The two teachers weren't sure what to do. When Herndon complained to the students, he was met with sneers and indignation. Wasn't it true that when he'd convinced them to sign up, he'd said that classes would be entirely open, that they could do whatever they wished? Herndon wrote, "I remind myself how things change when you give up your authority, officially, even if you really want to keep it, privately. The kids begin to talk to you just as if you are a real person, and often say just what they mean."[8] It was much easier, Herndon realized belatedly, to stay in the teacher–hero role.

To leave that role and support a new ideology created un-expected and not particularly glorious circumstances.

Herndon suggested, in fact, that he and Frank probably would have resorted to a traditional hard line if it hadn't been for three girls in the class. From the beginning they pursued the kind of project in which the teachers had hoped all the students would have become involved. They started a student newspaper called *Infinity*. While the other students ran around the halls, Meg would write articles, Lily would run off the paper and determine how to distribute it, and Jane would draw the illustrations.

These three girls represented Herndon's last hope for re-taining his original image of the class. He spoke with them, saying that he was going to compel the other students to participate in the newspaper. The girls adamantly disagreed. Couldn't they use the help, Herndon asked. Yes, they could use help, but they didn't want it under such conditions. It would be just like a regular journalism class, Meg said sneer-ingly. The main problem was that if other students were forced to work on *Infinity*, they would probably do a poor job. Bored people don't do good work, Meg explained. That was probably the reason why the journalism teacher ended up rewriting most of the material intended for the official school paper. No, students should only participate if they wished.

The teachers gave in. The permanent hall passes were con-tinued. Many students spent much of the class roaming the halls, and the class remained in a state of chaos by normal standards. Gradually, however, interest and involvement in the production of *Infinity* increased. When an issue was to be put together, everyone was alerted. Many of the students ar-rived in class that day prepared to collate the pages, staple them, and serve as runners for their distribution. Then they would sit down, read the paper, and discuss it, criticizing it and assessing its quality compared to earlier editions. Fur-thermore interest developed outside the class.

The offers came from other kids in other classes. They did exist. Stories poured in. There were secret writers all over the place. Kids in [the class] read them and judged them. *Infinity* kept coming out. The whole class took credit for it, time and time again, and they were right. *We* are doing it, they said. After all, who else was?[9]

An important point about this discussion is that it shows how delicate the process of encouraging creativity and autonomy among students is likely to be. In principle Herndon was a strong advocate of these two qualities, but when faced with the confusion and even chaos his experiment created, he was quite ready to cave in and be just as repressive as traditional educators. After all, he himself was a product of educational exclusionism. Only the efforts of three students stopped him.

## THE CURRENT EDUCATIONAL PLIGHT

Herndon received quite a bit of criticism from school officials for what he was doing. Today his colleagues, with the ready consent of parents, might have slit his throat. In the past decade, there has been a strong ideological shift "back to basics," back to traditional exclusionism in education. Teachers, administrators, parents, and employers have complained that students' basic skills are being less and less effectively developed in the schools. Some investigations support this conclusion. For instance, in April 1983, the National Commission on Excellence in Education issued a report on the state of American education. The Commission indicated that unless significant reform occurred, the nation would be seriously endangered in the future. The report emphasized that a number of other nations are overtaking the once unchallenged American lead in science, technology, commerce, and industry. The report, which was entitled *A Nation at Risk*, specifically highlighted a number of serious problems:

- Twenty-three million American adults are functionally illiterate;
- about thirteen percent of American adolescents are functionally illiterate;

- between 1963 and 1980, there was a steady decline in average scores on the Scholastic Aptitude Test (SAT);
- the number of remedial mathematics courses offered in public four-year colleges increased seventy-two percent between 1975 and 1980.[10]

Fear that the quality of education is declining has encouraged emphasis on going back to basics, with its focus on orthodox classroom performance, especially effective performance on standardized tests. The development of such skills is quite the antithesis of an emphasis on creativity and autonomy in learning. The James Herndons of the world now find that they're back in the less-than-happy days of the conformity-ridden 1950s, expected once again to promote little more than the values and skills that will help students succeed in modern capitalist America.

Most likely the renewed emphasis on going back to basics is a prominent reason why perhaps no generation of students has been as bored and disillusioned as the present one. Pamela Bardo, who gave up teaching high school after seventeen years, wrote an article in which she discussed her feelings about teachers' loss of enthusiasm for their jobs—what is known as "teacher burnout." Bardo explained that she could put up with her pupils arriving late, forgetting their supplies, sneaking out of class, and cheating on exams. Such behavior, Bardo emphasized, has always been typical of high school students. Then she added, "What I encountered in recent years was much more disturbing, even frightening. In increasing numbers, teenagers have begun using their ultimate weapon against the school, the teachers, and themselves: They are simply refusing to do the work that leads to learning."[11]

One might read Bardo's statement and conclude that, after all, she was a disillusioned teacher simply looking for an excuse to quit. However, the problem she cited is perceived to exist across the country. In a nationwide survey conducted in 1986, a Gallup Poll found that 24 percent of the informants indicated that lack of discipline was believed to be the biggest problem facing schools in their communities. Use of drugs ran first at 28 percent[12]—a problem that in many instances undoubtedly is linked to lack of discipline and, perhaps even more to the point, lack of clear direction. For many modern students and teachers, schools have become cultural ghost towns. These days the participants often restrict themselves to the most narrowly defined duties. Dullness prevails, and even when the hallways are crowded, schools seem lifeless and empty.

## COMMENTARY

Several years ago my wife and I went to Plymouth Village, where there is a row of authentic-looking cottages meant to be accurate representations of the original Plymouth Village. What struck me as even more interesting than the cottages was the people inside them—actors and actresses schooled in the ways of the Pilgrims' era and dressed to play the parts of actual people from the original village. One point was emphasized before we entered the village: The "residents" would be happy to talk with us "outsiders," but we needed to understand that they were supposed to be living in the 1620s with the perspectives and limitations of that era.

Soon after arriving we entered a cottage just in time to hear a fellow outsider launch himself enthusiastically into a detailed explanation of his work: He was a computer programmer. It rapidly became clear to any listener that this man was convinced that his explanation was opening this new, wondrous world to his deprived, preindustrial listeners. The "residents" of the cottage, a couple, listened silently for perhaps two minutes. Then as the programmer pronounced the word "computer" for the tenth or twelfth time, the man turned excitedly to the woman and explained in his distinctly British accent, "Abigail, the man's into pewter." Most of us laughed, and we were spared any further explanation.

This was one, seemingly insignificant incident. Perhaps I am making too much of it, but it seems to me that it epitomizes what is wrong with our education system. The twentieth-century visitor was probably well skilled in computer trade, but he lacked the vibrant imagination of a four-year-old. He was a well-finished product of an education system that, since the days of Horace Mann's narrow covenant with economic and political leaders, has provided an ideology encouraging people's involvement in the economy while also promoting an uncreative and unimaginative outlook on the world.

## SUMMARY

The original advocates of American public education established a covenant with the political and economic leadership, developing an exclusionist ideology emphasizing the virtues of capitalism in exchange for financial support. Since then, students have been carefully controlled in school and encouraged to become docile, bland citizens. Because of these deficiencies, many social analysts have sharply criticized American education. At the same time, as James Herndon's effort demonstrates, educational reform is difficult to accomplish. The current educational plight is highlighted by such reports as *A Nation at Risk*. With the current back-to-basics emphasis, it is not surprising that there is widespread teacher burnout. At the moment Horace Mann's exclusionist covenant seems likely to survive in the years ahead.

# 6

# The Bureaucratic Battlefield

Toward the end of the 1960s protests, I was looking for my first teaching job. Three people were present at the interview—the dean, the departmental chairman, and I.

It began as a fairly relaxed, innocuous discussion about the school and about my background. Then the dean brought up an incident that clearly was troubling him. One of his faculty members had initiated a number of protests. The dean turned to me: "You wouldn't think of doing that, would you?"

"Doing exactly what, sir?" In the context "that" was not really precise enough for a full, malicious enjoyment of the situation.

"Starting disruptive protests in the classroom?"

"No, sir, I definitely won't start disruptive protests in the classroom." Perhaps I would start one in a public place, I thought to myself, but not in the classroom.

At the time it was a bit difficult not to smile. The two men both seemed terribly serious, and I was young and taken with the gaucheness of the question. I was also flattered; I left the interview feeling a bit like a revolutionary.

Years later I am still struck by the gaucheness of the question, but my focus has enlarged. It is now apparent that, while acting clumsily, the dean was just doing his job, which required him to be a velvet-gloved extension of the campus police force. His college was looking for young, energetic teachers, but above all they had to hire people who would stick to the standard covenants—obey all important regulations and always maintain business as usual. In the 1960s such ideologies were being challenged in colleges and universities, and thus the enforcers had a tough job. It is easier now.

I will now discuss bureaucracies and bureaucratic activity. There is a widespread tendency to believe that people in bureaucracies are narrow-minded, dull, servile, and conformity-oriented as well as callous and even vindictive toward their opponents. In the present context, it is probably more useful to shift the focus from bureaucrats' personalities to the motivation for their actions—the idea of exclusionism. They are protecting their turf, keeping themselves secure in straightforward, decently paying jobs.

In this chapter I will examine the ideology of bureaucratic exclusionism and also the negative impact of bureaucratic procedures on people.

## THE BUREAUCRATIC IDEOLOGY: BUSINESS AS USUAL

The term "bureaucracy" is used loosely in our society. To help specify the meaning of bureaucracy, one can distinguish between an organization and a bureaucracy. Organizations, such as schools, hospitals, courts, corporations, and government agencies, are groups characterized by formally stated rules, clearly defined member roles, and distinct objectives. As organizations become larger and more complex, they need "bureaucracies"—organizations' administrative sections— which have the task of controlling their operation. Students, for example, are part of the organization of a school, but they are not part of its bureaucracy, because they have no administrative duties.

One might ask, if bureaucracies are often composed of people doing distasteful jobs, why not simply disband them? The barrier to doing that, of course, is that modern societies could not function without them. They are essential for keeping our organizations in running order, and without those organizations a vast number of critical tasks simply would not get done. Consequently, even though disbanding bureaucracies has a vague appeal for many of us, that idea has to be scrapped.

Actually analysts of bureaucracies have not always been critical of them. When Max Weber wrote about bureaucracies early in the twentieth century, he expressed admiration for their highly efficient, rational handling of administrative tasks. Bureaucratic characteristics, which enhance this efficiency, he indicated, include the specialization of workers, impersonality toward clients (who are supposed to be treated impartially as cases), and elaborate rules.[1] Weber was probably correct. These characteristics can make bureaucracies efficient. However, these same qualities can encourage employees to be dull, conforming, and occasionally vicious toward outsiders. Referring to the organizational structure produced in Puritan times, Arthur Miller suggested that it "was forged for a necessary propose and accomplished that purpose. But all organization is and must be grounded on the idea of exclusion and prohibition, just as two objects cannot occupy the same space."[2] Robert Merton offered a similar idea, emphasizing that within organizations, officials frequently develop a "bureaucratic personality," becoming immersed in bureaucratic procedures and frequently losing sight of organizational goals which might entail greater commitment and personal risk.[3]

## Whyte's "Organization Man" Perspective

How do bureaucracies lock people in? In *The Organization Man*, William H. Whyte, Jr., discussed an ideology prevalent in the workplace. One of its elements is "belongingness," the fervent desire to be a part of an organization. This desire is very strong, Whyte argued, because in modern society the family, church, community, and schools have failed to give individuals the sense of belonging for which they yearn. According to its advocates, belongingness has become a means to reestablish the security and comfort that existed in the Middle Ages when every worker knew his or her place. Whyte summarized the advocates' position:

What with the Enlightenment, the Industrial Revolution, and other calamities, the job is immensely more difficult than it was in those simpler days.... What we must do is to learn consciously to achieve what once came naturally. We must form an elite of skilled leaders who will guide men back, benevolently, to group belongingness.[4]

This "elite of skilled leaders," then, is supposed to provide benevolent guidance within organizations and their bureaucracies. Just like men in traditional families and teachers in traditional classrooms, bureaucratic leaders have the opportunity to become local heroes.

Another element in the organization man's ideology is what Whyte has called "togetherness." In seeking to belong, the organization man pursues togetherness, trying to immerse himself in a variety of group experiences within the organization. This may be found in the exchanges at the conference table, the seminar, the workshop, or in the after-hours discussion group.

Why is there such enthusiasm for togetherness? Whyte believed that there have been two sources. One has been the premature conclusion that the group is invariably mightier than the individual. While the accuracy of this conclusion has not been firmly established, there is a large body of continuing research that endorses it. Acting on the belief that the conclusion is correct, attempts have been made to determine principles of group functioning.

The second reason for supporting togetherness involves morality. Advocates of this position believe that if they back togetherness, then egotistical tendencies will be deemphasized and the best qualities of members will inevitably appear in group activities. Whyte has not been happy with such a position. He pointed out that most group efforts which try to maximize agreement among members tend to downplay individuals' originality and creativity. In committee meetings, for example, people often feel a strong impulse to seek common ground with their fellow members. They "tend to soft-pedal that which would go against the grain. And that, unfortunately, can include unorthodox ideas."[5]

## Janis's "Groupthink" Approach

The picture that emerges from Whyte's book is that bureaucrats tend to huddle together, believing that belongingness and togetherness are very desirable goals. Any course of action that fails to emphasize those two conditions is simply rejected. It is not a comforting conclusion for anyone seeking signs of individual courage, autonomy, or creativity in bureaucracies. Irving Janis's *Victims of Groupthink* offers no respite from such a perspective.

In 1972 Janis, a social psychologist, published a book in which he analyzed principles governing decision making in the foreign-policy area. Reading the book, one is impressed by the extent to which exclusionism prevailed in decision making, with the wisdom or common sense of both outsiders and insiders ruled out if it was not consistent with leaders' positions.

One of Janis's case studies—the abortive effort to invade Cuba at the Bay of Pigs—illustrates how the "groupthink" process works. To begin, Janis pointed out that one of the basic factors in groupthink situations is the illusion of invulnerability. If the leader and other group members believe that a plan will work, then any possible dangers or drawbacks will not be taken seriously. In this instance the impact of the illusion of invulnerability was magnified by the fact that the decision to invade Cuba was made by President John Kennedy, who, to put it mildly, was "on a roll" at the time. In the past year, he had won the nomination and the election against strong odds. He was the "Wonder Boy," and was believed by all around him to have an unfailing Midas touch.

Another characteristic of the groupthink process is an illusion of unanimity. In the Bay of Pigs case, there was very little expression of dissent about the invasion plan. Kennedy and the other leaders assumed that because there was no criticism, all the participants were in favor of the plan. This was hardly the case. Secretary of State Dean Rusk, for example, had strong doubts about its practicality. He expressed these doubts in State Department meetings, which he ran, but in the presidential advisory group he restricted himself to gentle warnings about avoiding excesses.

Those who participate in groupthink often suppress personal misgivings. They do this because they do not want to cast doubt on a decision which they feel has already been approved by the group. After the Bay of Pigs invasion was thwarted, Arthur Schlesinger, an under secretary of state, berated himself for having failed to express his doubts in the meetings just before the invasion. However, he comforted himself with the realization that a few timid objections would have done nothing more than create an image of him as a nuisance.

Another important ingredient in the groupthink process is the existence of what Janis called "mindguards." Mindguards, like bodyguards, are individuals who protect someone important. A mindguard's activity might be more subtle than that of the physical counterpart, but basically it is similar. At one point Bobby Kennedy, the president's brother and chief mindguard, became aware of Schlesinger's doubts about the invasion plan. At a party Kennedy took Schlesinger aside and after hearing an explanation of his position said, "You may be right or you may be wrong, but the President has made his mind up. Don't push it any further. Now is the time for everyone to help him all they can."[6] This statement came from an important, intelligent man whose ethical code generally required that he permit and even encourage freedom of dissent. However, he was not about to encourage it in this instance.

Another element common to groupthink situations is what Janis has called "docility fostered by suave leadership." The leaders—in this case Kennedy and his closest advisors—carefully orchestrated the presentation of dissent. Shortly after newspapers had printed stories indicating that the United States had plans for invading Cuba, President Kennedy asked Senator J. William Fullbright to speak to him and his advisors. Fullbright gave a strong speech, correctly predicting many of the damaging effects the invasion would have on

American foreign policy. Following the speech Kennedy forsook the conventional pattern of asking for questions and comments. Instead he took a straw poll, asking each advisor present to indicate whether or not he supported the invasion. In the course of the voting, an individual made a procedural point that interested Kennedy, and he opened discussion on the issue. By this time the moral and political issues Fullbright had raised were effectively obscured. Kennedy terminated the meeting before the straw poll was completed. Whether it was intended or not, the meeting ended before Schlesinger, the one man who might have voted against the plan, had a chance to state his position.

John Kennedy was a genuine hero to many Americans, including the intelligent, sophisticated men who were his closest advisors. Men like Arthur Schlesinger and Dean Rusk might have had some personal doubts about the Bay of Pigs invasion but probably felt that as "mere mortals," they could not oppose this heroic man of destiny. They too let themselves be swept along.

With the concept of groupthink in mind, how would one expect bureaucrats to respond if called upon to offer advice in a dangerous, unclear situation? I will consider a recent case. In May 1985, four days before the mayor of Philadelphia approved a police plan to drop a bomb on a row house occupied by a radical group, he met with his closest advisors. They barely opened their mouths. Later the district attorney commented, "There was . . . dread in that room you could cut with a knife."[7] These were people used to making fairly simple, safe decisions about city policy. They were not equipped either intellectually or emotionally for confronting questions about life and death. If that group had been able to generate an intelligent discussion where all options were examined and evaluated, then eleven people might not have been killed nor a neighborhood destroyed.

## The Concept of Dynamic Stagnation

Another bureaucratic process is what I have called "dynamic stagnation." This is an intricate and at times heartrending process; it is heartrending because the bureaucratic leaders have some truly altruistic aims which they themselves undermine. Dynamic stagnation generally occurs only in nonprofit organizations, which thus permit their members to have an additional priority besides making money. Let us consider what happens.

The bureaucratic leaders claim that the organization is committed to an ideology that is collective and perhaps revolutionary. In the federally funded antipoverty agency that I studied in the late 1960s, the ideology emphasized the importance of successful community action, meaning that members of the local poor communities would be mobilized to seek improvements in work opportunities, education, and a variety of local services. Generally those spearheading community action find it necessary to constantly oppose the local power structure in order to accomplish their goals.

When dynamic stagnation occurs, leaders emphasize the priority of the collective task, but they spend little time engaged in it. There are two reasons why this is the case. First, the activity is tough, with little or no short-term payoff. Second, it is recognized that the tenacious pursuit of this goal will mean a head-to-head confrontation with many local individuals and groups (including powerful people) who would be adversely affected by its accomplishment. In the case of the agency I studied, successful community action would have meant that the city would have had to allot a much larger portion of its budget to meet the needs of the poor. This, of course, would have meant the transfer of funds from other civic priorities or an increase in local taxes. Neither approach would have received widespread public support.

In such situations bureaucratic leaders are in a difficult position. They have a cherished goal, but its staunch pursuit will insure their downfall. What should they do? The course of action gradually becomes clear: Don't pursue the dangerous goal but obscure the failure to act. There are two means to accomplish this.

First, certain secondary, less volatile tasks can absorb staff members' time and energy and, if these are performed effectively, little opportunity will remain for the primary goal. In the agency I studied, the workers spent about ninety percent of their time helping individuals and families with a variety of housing, job, medical, educational, and legal problems. More than anything else, the staff acted as intermediaries between clients and the long-established agencies, which were supposed to supply specific services. As one worker told me: "It turns out that our job is to be watchdogs, making sure that the welfare department, the housing department, the schools, and the courts do right by our people."[8] Over the year and a half of my research, the steadily growing volume of requests for this kind of assistance was testimony to the staff members' effectiveness.

The second way to conceal the gap between the stated priority of a goal and its actual deemphasis is to claim that certain powerful individuals related to the organization are dangerous adversaries and are hampering its success. In many instances these claims are more than a ruse; the bureaucratic leaders believe their own words of indictment. In the antipoverty agency, there was a board of directors meeting every other Thursday evening. The next morning at the weekly staff meeting the leaders would often spend an inordinate amount of time going over the details of the previous night's meeting and pointing out how this or that powerful individual had made a seemingly benign comment which had frightening or even cataclysmic implications. Then the director would usually make a statement like the following one: "If we don't get control over the most dangerous board members, then we'll never be able to get on top of community action."[9]

Neither I nor the majority of the staff could see the connection between "controlling" board members and the successful performance of community action. In fact, it was never clear to me just what "controlling" board members meant. Most of the staff members felt that these prolonged analyses of board members were boring and nonproductive. I am convinced, however, that in a special sense they were productive. The agency leaders had to believe that some board members were dangerous and required control. It was this belief that held them in a delicate balance, still performing safe activities while keeping themselves one step away from having to jeopardize their jobs and reputations by engaging in community action. It was an unending, dynamic struggle simply to keep the status quo, that is stagnation. That is why I have called the process "dynamic stagnation."

Years later an image that often comes to mind is the elegant, talented, articulate director turning to me one day and saying with a feeble, self-mocking laugh, "You know, when I wake up in the morning, I'm never sure what hat I'll be wearing that day. It's like someone's playing games with me."[10]

Perhaps in a way that is just what was happening. This woman and her fellow leaders in the agency were working hard to maintain an image of themselves as the guardians and heroes of the local poor, but they were not able to observe the presence of an insidious trickster—the same self-protective exclusionism found in more prosaic bureaucracies.

## BUREAUCRACY AS A MORAL ISSUE: WHO LOSES?

So far we have seen that bureaucrats are often narrow-minded, self-interested, and sometimes confused, but little about the impact of their activities has been suggested. In a recent paper, Sjoberg, Vaughan, and Williams concluded that bureaucratic activity often produces two morally suspect situations—secretive activity and the exploitation of disadvantaged people. On the first issue, it greatly facilitated Nazi leaders' genocidal activities to be able to carry them out secretly. If the issue of genocide seems far removed from modern life, it should be emphasized that a major stumbling block to the resolution of the arms race is the problem of mutual accountability—the difficulty, if not the impossibility of developing procedures to assure that both Soviet and American government bureaucrats are not secretly carrying out plans or procedures to get an arms advantage over the other side.

On the second topic, Sjoberg, Vaughan, and Williams suggested that while bureaucratic standards emphasize fair and equal treatment, disadvantaged people benefit less readily from such standards than others. For instance, in educational or job training programs, most people from lower-class backgrounds enter such programs with limited relevant skills and usually do not have a chance to catch up sufficiently to survive in such programs. Furthermore, because of the bureaucratic personality's narrow perspective, those who fail tend to receive the brunt of the blame for their failure. Little or no effort is made to understand the source of their failure or, above all, to alter the conditions that produced it.[11]

## A CONCLUDING COMMENT

Recently I was walking my dog early in the morning, and as I was about to return home, I looked up the street and saw two patrol cars and nearby an officer talking to a man. Being an incurably curious soul, I walked up to a patrolman sitting in one of the cars drinking coffee. I knocked on the window, and he rolled it down. "What's going on here?" I asked. He barely looked at me. "Oh, nothing, nothing. Everything's fine," he replied.

It seemed wisest to repress all smart comments, and so I just walked away. Thinking back on the exchange, I concede that not telling me what was going on might have been a sound decision. What I object to, however, is the style. Couldn't the patrolman have detached himself from bureaucratic regulations sufficiently to have said, "Look, I'm not at liberty to supply details, but let me assure you that it's nothing major"? On the surface that seems so easy to do, but in a world where bureaucracies tend to encourage narrow, self-protective responses, it is going to take some significant reform before police and others will be inclined to respond differently.

I would like to think that such incidents are unusual, but I am certain they are commonplace. Bureaucracies tend to have authoritarian structures and ideologies, and there is no indication that this trend is changing. My guess is that if the open covenant becomes a reality, career bureaucrats will be among the last to embrace it, and because of the narrow, rule-oriented nature of their world, their embrace will be nothing more than a cold, formal acknowledgment.

## SUMMARY

This chapter began with a definition of bureaucracy and a brief discussion of Weber's essay on the functions of bureaucracy. Then I examined three critical outlooks on bureaucratic activity, analyzing that topic with the concepts of the organization man, groupthink, and dynamic stagnation. I also discussed the destructive impact of bureaucracy on people's lives. Throughout the chapter it was emphasized that bureaucracies have authoritarian structures and ideologies.

These last three chapters have focused on exclusionist ideologies in three major structures—the family, schools, and bureaucracies. Now we see that in spite of the pervasiveness of exclusionism in American society, there are some indications that this condition is beginning to recede.

# 7

# The Slow Thaw

I was employed as a consultant for a major survey firm. One of the job's chief assets was that several times a week the boss and I plunged into a freewheeling discussion about survey data. About an hour into one discussion, he pointed a finger at me and said, "Tell me. What do you think has been the clearest trend I've observed in the American people in forty years of survey research?"

I thought for a minute. "Something about race relations?"

"No, but you're on the right track. It's broader than that."

I shook my head.

"O.K. Ever since World War II, survey data on the American people have shown that they've become increasingly tolerant of each other's values, beliefs, and lifestyle. The average American seems to be saying,"I might not want to marry into so-and-so's family, believe what he or she does, or live as that person does, but I sure-as-hell support his or her right to full participation in American society.' "

"Did this trend accelerate during the 1960s?"

"No, not especially. It's a relentless pattern over a forty-year period."

In 1981 I had this conversation with one of the nation's leading survey specialists. While the 1980s has been widely labeled a conservative era, I will demonstrate shortly that there is evidence of the same trend in the present decade.

One should not misunderstand: I am not suggesting that

the golden age is about to descend upon us from heaven. Our society will continue to produce cruelty, bigotry, stupidity, and callousness; that likelihood has been stressed in previous chapters. What I am suggesting here is a single significant point: that there has been a type of slow thaw, a gradual ideological shift emphasizing increasingly tolerant social relations between different groups in this country.

My suspicion is that the tolerance issue is just the visible tip of the iceberg. As the material in this chapter suggests, there has been a trend over the past four decades to examine a variety of social issues with a depth and compassion that was lacking in the past. Without this thaw the development of the open covenant would not be possible.

## AMERICAN VALUES AND HUMANITARIANISM

In chapter 3 I noted that Americans have values stressing achievement and hard work, but that the American culture also contains some very different values, which are consistent with increasing tolerance. According to Robin Williams, Jr., there has always been a humanitarian tendency in Americans—an inclination to support the underdog, to show "impulsive sympathy" for people in distress, to become angry at groups and individuals that are overbearing, and to take pride in the nation as a haven for the homeless and downtrodden. A broad and persistent belief in the relationship of all humanity underlies the enormous range of relatively disinterested humanitarian activities in the United States—the United Fund, "service club" activities, public welfare agencies, private philanthropies, and others.[1]

Perhaps even more to the point has been the American emphasis on equality, especially equality of opportunity. Although there were systems of inequality brought to this land from Europe, the American colonies in comparison were relatively free of structured social inequalities. The reasons included the looseness of English political control; the relatively modest social-class origins of most colonists, which encouraged most of them to reject the rigid class distinctions of their parent societies; and the availability of rich land and other natural resources, which permitted all free citizens to develop personal wealth and reject the European feudal systems. Williams indicated that "until the late nineteenth century, America was able to develop without having to face widespread conflict between the principle of equality and the principles of achievement and freedom. In this historical experience, through generation after generation, the values of equality were crystallized and elaborated."[2]

The crystallization and elaboration of equality were slow processes, however. As recently as the beginning of the twentieth century, bigotry, racism, and intolerance ran rampant. In 1906 Mark Twain attended a banquet where a speaker received thunderous applause when he fervently told his audience of lawyers, bankers, and other middle-class professionals, "We are of the Anglo-Saxon race, and when the Anglo-Saxon wants a thing *he just takes it*."[3] That was at the beginning of this century, within the lifetime of millions of elderly citizens. It was not until the late 1950s that there occurred anything approaching an organized attack on Americans' intolerance.

## THE BEAT ERA

Actually the attack on intolerance was not very organized at first. During the "happy days" of the middle 1950s, the beats, a group of young, angry artistic men and women, who had broken with their families' respectable, middle-class way of life, launched virulent criticisms of American society. The best known of the beats was the writer Jack Kerouac. The title of his most famous novel—*On the Road*—suggests the beats' rootlessness and restless wandering. Only by being rootless and putting oneself in jeopardy, they believed, could a person see the raw truth of life. Sal Paradise, the narrator of *On the Road*, offered this illustration:

> That night in Harrisburg I had to sleep in the railroad station on a bench; at dawn the station masters threw me out. Isn't it true that you start your life a sweet child believing in everything under your father's roof? Then

comes the day ... when you know you are wretched and miserable and poor and blind and naked, and with the visage of a gruesome grieving ghost you go shuddering through nightmare life.[4]

Kerouac felt that life on the road allowed people to see the banal reality of American life. All winter Sal Paradise had read about the glory of the Old West, but when he arrived in one historic area, all he saw was "cute suburban cottages of one damn kind and another"[5] In another celebrated place there were no people resembling the cowboys of the Old West, only "fat businessmen in boots and ten-gallon hats, with their hefty wives in cowgirl attire, [who] bustled and whooped on the wooden side-walks."[6]

As Sal Paradise changed physical locales, he also conducted an inner journey of self-examination and questioning. When he walked through the black section of Denver, he realized that the white world didn't give him enough, "not enough ecstasy for me, not enough life, joy, kicks, darkness, music, not enough night."[7] It would be better, he decided, to be a local Mexican or even a poor, overworked Japanese laborer, than to be a dreary, disillusioned white man.

The beats did not offer any solutions, and they did not actively protest, but the questions they raised and the criticisms they provided set a foundation for the 1960s countercultural protests. What the beats did was important: They ripped away at traditional heroes, lifestyles, and exclusionist ideology. It is always easier for voices of dissent to have an impact when someone else has previously raised similar themes.

## THE 1960s COUNTERCULTURAL PROTESTS

For me the first striking memory of the 1960s occurred several years before the protests, in 1960. I was a sophomore in a political science course that contained many of the most politically active students on what was then a politically active campus. One day the instructor explained that while some Americans were inclined to protest domestic government policy, it was the American tradition to stand united behind the president and other government officials when they took positions on international issues. The instructor's statement was met with silence. This was a class of activists, some of whom would argue almost anything, and yet not a hint of objection was expressed.

Through the past quarter-century, the eloquence of that silence has deepened for me. What happened, or did not happen in that classroom makes it abundantly clear how different the spirit of the opening year of that decade was from the spirit of the years toward its end. Starting in 1965, hundreds of thousands of young people launched an attack on traditional American values, in particular exclusionist standards of patriotism, racism, and eventually sexism.

For most of those years the attack was directed against traditional patriotism. The central issue was the Vietnam War. At public protests throughout the country, male college students chanted their refusal to go to war: "Hell No! We won't go!" It was an assault on the patriotic tradition declaring that when the government calls, young men should be willing to go and die for their country without question. The Vietnam War, the protesters said, was "an unjust war," and went on to say that it is not heroic but instead is tragically senseless to die for one's country in an unjust war. "America, your country, love it or leave it!" was the retort from traditional patriots, who were fervent supporters of exclusionism. Go along with government policy, they urged, because that policy represents the country. To oppose the government, especially in time of war, is unpatriotic, and more than that, it's treasonous. The long-haired overprivileged protesters, the traditionalists declared, were nothing but communist traitors who received their orders from Moscow, and they demanded that the protestors should get out of "God's country" and leave the rest of the hard-working, patriotic Americans, who appreciated the privilege of being Americans, to carry on with their shoulders squared and their heads held high.

During the late sixties, it was frequently suggested that the American people were more sharply divided than at any time since the Civil War. Because there were no surveys in those years, we cannot make any direct comparisons. Modern polling results, however, do show that profound cleavages existed during the Vietnam War. When asked in March 1969 what the United States should do next in regard to the Vietnam situation, 32 percent of a national sample said go all-out to win, 26 percent said pull out, 19 percent said work for a cease-fire at the Paris peace talks (and stay in Vietnam until those negotiations were completed), 19 percent said simply end the war as soon as possible, and 4 percent gave other opinions.[8] This was quite a range of different opinions. By May 1971, when asked whether the United States made a mistake sending troops to fight in Vietnam, 61 percent of a national sample said yes, 28 percent replied no, and 11 percent offered no opinion.[9]

The unblemished American war record—six wins and no defeats (overlooking the "police action" in Korea, and the Civil War, which might be considered a no-holds-barred scrimmage)—now had an indisputable "1" in the loss column. Furthermore, as the second survey item above shows, it was a war that a distinct majority of Americans in retrospect considered a mistake.

As many Americans began to question their leaders' decisions, they also began to question the esteem in which they had held those leaders. Political leaders who had been heroes to many were now seen as fallible or even despicable. For the more ardent protesters, those feelings even included the prominent liberal leaders. This was brought home to me in the spring of 1967, during a discussion with a local student leader about a teach-in that was being organized. "Since Bobby Kennedy is our senator, I don't think we'd have much trouble getting him to attend," someone said.

"That would be great, a real coup," someone else suggested.

The student leader shook his head. "I don't agree. Kennedy's not so bad, but what could he offer us? He's not a radical, not committed to work outside the system to bring change. We need someone who's been willing to put his body on the line for a cause. We won't find that among the political leadership."

A search was on for new heroes, people who could break with exclusionism, look beyond traditional ideologies, and seek to develop new ones. In his book about the lives of ten sixties activists, J. Anthony Lukas included an account of what happened to Sue Thrasher, a Southern white woman who became an organizer for civil rights and antiwar activity. During this period of her life, Sue struggled to understand the social world around her. She hated exclusionism, especially the racism and bigotry which she had observed since childhood; she felt that there was much more to Southern life. She studied country music, and she sang it. She talked with long-term Southern labor movement people about their work. She visited the home of Sam Reece, once a prominent labor organizer, and Sam and his wife Florence talked about the parallels between the union fight and the sixties movement. Sue was particularly impressed with Florence, feeling that she had been through her own struggle and as a result had a clear understanding of what blacks in the South were experiencing. Lukas wrote:

> People like the Reeces were terribly important to Sue because she had never rejected the rural Southerner. "I rejected the out-and-out racists, the Klansmen, the women who shouted dirty names at Negro children going to school. They were my enemies. But I could never reject the average white Southerner, because that would have meant turning against my family. I always believed that there were deep reservoirs of very decent, good, even radical feelings in many Southerners which could be tapped if only we worked hard enough."[10]

The 1960s countercultural protests were important benchmarks in recent American history. In their aftermath it is likely that traditional, exclusionist values will never again be firmly reinstated. It is important, however, not to focus entirely on the events themselves. Had these events not occurred, it is still likely that American society would have been developing new attitudes toward social issues in recent years because of the nature of that society.

This is a late-industrial society, which means it contains a highly developed system of education and a highly diversified mass media. In spite of the limitations discussed in chapter 6, education elicits many ideas that are potentially subversive, encouraging people to challenge the status quo. Because of the potentially subversive impact of education, slave owners did not want their slaves to learn to read; this quality of education is probably one of the unarticulated but underlying reasons for the ongoing conflict about what is taught in the schools. In the 1960s the subversive quality was readily apparent, but it is still an ever-present possibility for teachers who encourage students to think independently and creatively.

Modern mass media provide the means of dispersing information about anything that happens, as long as it is considered newsworthy. Accounts of protests were often splashed on newspapers, magazines, and television screens across the country and even around the world. Furthermore, with the wealth of resources available in this country, leftist groups and organizations have been able to start their own magazines and newspapers. Some, like *New Republic* and *Nation*, had been publishing for decades before the 1960s and survived after that era, but others, like *The Minority of One*, *Ramparts*, or *Liberation*, started and eventually died during that time.

## THE CENTERED-ON-SELF SEVENTIES

The 1970s was often disparagingly referred to as the "me decade." Admittedly, following the 1960s protests, many of the prominent seventies activities seemed individualistic and self-centered, yet it is likely that the "me decade" designation has been quite inaccurate. Some of the 1970s activity was not so much self-centered as centered-on-self-development, with an emphasis on meditation, relaxation, and spiritual growth, which had roots in Eastern philosophies and religions.

Such efforts tend to be focused on the intimate interrelation between all people, or actually among all living things. The fact that many of those who pursued spiritual growth were often not very successful and soon gave up the hunt is hardly surprising; our rational, competitive society makes the quest for spiritual growth a highly elusive activity. In Robert Pirsig's *Zen and the Art of Motorcycle Maintenance*, a novel which was very popular in the middle 1970's, the protagonist undertook two journeys: one across the country by motorcycle with his son, and the other within himself—an inner journey of self-discovery in which the hero tried to reconcile his past absorption in Eastern philosophy with his current life in the Western world. As the travellers literally and figuratively rode west, the man pondered things that had happened to him at earlier times. He recalled the days when he had travelled with some black artists, who constantly accused him of intellectualizing everything. He, in turn, tried to pin them down on just what they meant. Finally one of his friends said, "Man, will you just please, kindly *dig* it . . . and hold up on all those wonderful seven-dollar questions? If you got to ask what *is* all the time, you'll never get time to *know*."[11]

Years later the man had accepted this conclusion. He had become fixated on a concept, which he called "Quality." Quality, though never actually defined in the book, seems to be a wholly nonrational, and thus spiritual, commitment to an enterprise. With the use of this concept, the man contended, all human activity could be dichotomized: "You take your analytic knife, put the point directly on the term Quality and just tap, not hard, gently, and the world splits, cleaves, right in two—hip and square, . . . technological and humanistic."[12]

Big deal, one might say. The fact that some man back in the seventies wrote a best-seller about Americans' spiritual search doesn't mean a thing. We Americans are the most rational, competitive, aggressive people that ever lived: We are the epitome of everything that is not spiritual.

Certainly there has been evidence in this book (chapter 3 in particular) to support such a position. However, recent national survey data suggest another possible conclusion. When asked whether they have ever been aware of or influenced by a presence or power (whether they call it God or not) different from their everyday self, 43 percent of a national sample answered yes.

Women, people with more education, and those aged thirty to forty-nine reported a greater likelihood of having had spiritual experiences. Overall those who reported such experiences overwhelmingly felt that what had happened was positive: It bolstered the person's belief in God, it provided new strength for living, it made the individual a better person, or it generally had a positive effect.[13]

People's sense of a spiritual presence is one indicator of heightened spiritual experience. At a more mundane level, there is the desire to belong to a community. A leading survey firm has measured this dimension each year for over a decade. In 1973 this organization found that 32 percent (or roughly a third) of Americans felt an intense need to compensate for the impersonal and threatening aspects of modern life by seeking involvement with others based on close ethnic ties, shared interests, or similar needs, background, age, or values. By the end of the 1970s, the proportion of Americans involved in this so-called "search for community" had increased by nearly half, to 47 percent—a startling jump in just a six-year period.[14]

For me personally, the seventies ended with a question mark: What actions would individuals affected by heightened spiritualism and sense of community be inclined to take? It is difficult to know—perhaps it is similar to asking about the long-term impact of a certain type of schooling or religious training. I do suspect, however, that the lives of many individuals belonging to the three social movements discussed in the next chapter were significantly affected by spiritual experiences in the 1970s.

## THE EIGHTIES AND A DOUBLE TREND

I have already referred to the 1980s, suggesting that the trend of tolerance has carried into this decade. According to survey specialist Daniel Yankelovich, that is true, but it is only part of the story.

Interviewed in 1984 about young Americans' values, Yankelovich emphasized one conservative tendency and one liberal one. The conservative trend has been produced by tough economic and occupational conditions. Unlike the 1960s and early 1970s, this is not an affluent era. Young people attending school and seeking jobs find that they must prepare themselves carefully for specific slots. If they do not, they will not get the job they seek or, in fact, may get no job at all. "I have to play by the rules," modern young people are inclined to say. "Why shouldn't others?" In short, this is an era of tough realities. Young people aged eighteen to twenty-six are more inclined than those ten years older to support capital punishment, to oppose abortion as a means of eliminating an unwanted pregnancy, and to have confidence in the military.

On some issues, in contrast, the theme of tolerance emphasized in the 1960s has been sustained or even expanded. For instance, today's eighteen- to twenty-six-year-olds are more inclined than people twenty-seven to thirty-six to favor the busing of black and white children, and less likely to agree that it is more important for a wife to help her husband's career than to have one herself. Furthermore these two age categories share the most liberal position of all ages on two issues: Both age groups are equally inclined to conclude that homeowners should not refuse to sell homes to people because of race or color and equally likely to disagree that it is better for all involved if the man is the achiever outside the home and the woman takes care of home and family.[15]

The data just presented suggest that while there is some truth to the often-stated claim that the 1980s has been a decade of conservative retrenchment, this conclusion is an oversimplification. In certain areas, especially issues involving individual rights, the 1980s continues the "slow thaw" of the past four decades.

## COMMENTARY

To many, the "slow thaw" has often appeared maddingly slow, but at unexpected moments the advances seemed almost magical. Back in the early 1970s, a group of students at my college were protesting Nixon's invasion of Cambodia. There were a number of planning sessions in preparation for a large public meeting. Most of the planners were men, but two women also participated. Gradually one of the women assumed an increasingly larger role in the planning session. Nothing official was ever declared, but by the time the meeting occurred, it was generally accepted that she would run the event. She confidently took the microphone and strode out before more than a thousand of her contemporaries. In those days if men were involved, women simply did not run large protest meetings, but apparently that didn't faze her. At that moment I remember thinking to myself, "So this is how change occurs!"

## SUMMARY

I have argued that since World War II, there has been a "slow thaw," a gradual ideological shift emphasizing increasingly tolerant social relations and a willingness to examine social issues with a depth and compassion previously less prevalent. Evidence from the beat era of the 1950s, the countercultural protests of the 1960s, the self-development activities of the 1970s, and, somewhat surprisingly, an emphasis on individual rights in the 1980s, all support the trend.

Without the "slow thaw," the development of the three social movements discussed in the next chapter would either not have occurred or at least would have been much slower.

# 8

# The No-fault Strategy

In J. R. R. Tolkien's *The Lord of the Rings*, a number of hobbits, men, a dwarf, and an elf undertook a perilous journey. At one point the company reached the Naith of Lorien, an elfin kingdom. As they entered the kingdom, Haldir, the elfin guide, pointed out that it would be necessary to blindfold Gimli the dwarf.

Gimli protested, saying that he refused to be blindfolded like a beggar or prisoner. He was not a spy, and like the others his only concern was the defeat of their common enemies: "I am no more likely to betray you than Legolas [an elf], or any other of my companions."

Haldir replied that he didn't doubt Gimli's word but that it was a question of law, which he was in no position to set aside.

Gimli was angry. He said that he would go forward free or would return alone to his own land, if necessary risking death in the wilderness.

No, that wouldn't be possible, the guide declared sternly. Gimli had come this far. Along with the other members of the company, he needed to appear before the Lord and Lady of the Naith.

Gimli drew his axe. Haldir and his elvin companions bent their bows. "A plague on Dwarves and their stiff necks!" said Legolas.

Then Aragorn, the leader of the company, stepped in.

"If I am still to lead this Company, you must do as I bid. It is hard upon the Dwarf to be thus singled out. We will all be blindfold [sic], even Legolas. That will be best, though it will make the journey slow and dull."

Gimli laughed suddenly. "A merry troop of fools we shall look! Will Haldir lead us all on a string, like many blind beggars with one dog? But I be content, if only Legolas here shares my blindness."

"I am an Elf and a kinsman here," said Legolas, becoming angry in his turn.

"Now let us cry: 'a plague on the stiff necks of Elves!' " said Aragorn. "But the Company shall all fare alike. Come, bind our eyes, Haldir!"[1]


*The Lord of the Rings* concerns the struggle between good and evil, and scenes like this one gradually convey to the reader that to be good requires much more than wishful thinking: It takes an unrelenting on-the-job effort. One might consider that Aragorn was in some respects a heroic figure, but he is a very different kind of hero from conventional types: He recognized that in all disputes a standard of equality is useful or even necessary. Aragorn knew how to put into practice the ideas I am about to discuss.

"Perhaps this kind of analysis is interesting," a critic might comment, "but fiction is not the real world. In the real world things are really tough."

"Fair enough," the critic's critic might reply. "The real world is tough, but a realistic analysis reveals signs that some changes are occurring." Such a position is developed in the last three chapters of this book.

Central to the discussion is a new concept—the no-fault strategy. I will examine the meaning of the no-fault strategy; discuss its relationship to the women's movement, the environmental movement, and the antinuclear movement; and analyze what is called "the tragic nature" of the no-fault strategy.

## THE MEANING OF THE NO-FAULT STRATEGY

Those who embrace what I call "the no-fault strategy" accept the following conclusion: The most expedient course of action in a given situation is not to blame prospective opponents for wrongdoing but rather to accept that the most satisfactory solution for all concerned will only be reached if all participants share both responsibility and blame. "We're in this together," the proponents of the no-fault strategy say. "I might not like or admire the other guy, but we'd better figure out a way to get along. Otherwise we all lose." This course of action directly opposes exclusionist tendencies and is a significant step toward establishing an open covenant.

The concept of no-fault was first introduced with car insurance. When the California legislature passed no-fault divorce legislation in 1970, the concept was then employed in an area of social relations as well. No-fault divorce law breaks from traditional divorce law in several respects. First, it eliminates the fault-based grounds for divorce. No longer is it necessary to establish that one of the partners is "the bad guy," who has committed adultery or engaged in cruel behavior. The new standard focuses on "irreconcilable difference"; the focus of failure is the relationship, not the couple. Second, no-fault divorce is meant to curtail or eliminate the adversarial process. Since the partners no longer have reason to establish one partner's legal responsibility for the failure of the marriage, a primary reason for animosity is eliminated. Third, financial settlement is supposed to be determined by standards stressing equity and economic need. It is no longer considered appropriate to provide alimony and property as a reward for virtue or to withhold them as punishment for wrongdoing. Therefore a wife will probably not receive alimony if her earning power equals or exceeds her husband's. However, if she has devoted herself to homemaking and has not worked outside the home, she is unlikely to have other resources and is entitled to alimony. Each case, in short, is determined on its own merits.[2]

In this chapter, three major social issues of our time—the

recent phase of the modern women's movement, the environmental movement, and the antinuclear movement—have been chosen for examination because they illustrate a no-fault strategy. This point of view contains two basic qualities.

First, the no-fault strategy emphasizes the importance of participants' cooperation. The parties involved might not be friendly; they might even have a history of adversarial relations. However, they cannot afford to view each other as enemies, because enemies do not cooperate, and their particular goal can not be accomplished unless the cooperation of all engaged parties is obtained. The use of the no-fault strategy represents a step toward the establishment of open covenants, where disagreeing parties, often with diverse backgrounds and outlooks, will reach agreement on issues of great importance to all participants.

A second quality of the no-fault strategy is that, in any negotiation where participants maintain this outlook, those individuals consider each other as equals. This ideological stance recognizes that since the different parties are involved in a situation where only the cooperation of all can produce success, then the refusal of one or more to cooperate can produce failure. Perhaps there is no better way to assure failure than to create resentment among the participants. Such an outcome can be brought about easily by designating one party superior to another. The "slow thaw" of recent decades discussed in the last chapter is particularly significant because it has encouraged people to see others with different characteristics as equals. Heroes, however, tend to consider themselves and their supporters as superiors, not equals to groups with which they must deal. Thus this particular issue suggests the obsolescence of heroes in no-fault situations.

Cooperation and equality of participants are basic qualities of a no-fault strategy. Another characteristic that seems to be common, if not inherent to the pattern, is the prominent involvement of women. Over the past several decades, an increasing proportion of women have received extensive education and obtained prestigious, high-paying jobs. At the same time, I suspect, many of them have been able to retain much of the traditionally emphasized female ability to perceive others' emotional needs. My conviction is that overall women tend to be considerably better at this skill than men because it is a skill that traditionally has been considered neither masculine nor heroic. Women have been more concerned about others' needs and less concerned about the achievement of narrow goals—in short, less exclusionist.

### Closure and the No-fault Strategy

During the early 1950s, Edwin Lemert developed a sociological theory about check forging. He suggested that men with certain characteristics—white, middle-class, and uninitiated in crime—are inclined to turn to check forging when they need money quickly and are unable to obtain it from other sources. Loneliness and isolation promote the process by driving these men to gambling, womanizing, or other activities that require large sums of money and creating a situation where they have little chance to seek other opinions regarding the morality and feasibility of their course of action. Lemert's perspective is a closure theory because alternatives to a particular choice are "closed" off. The alternatives do not seem, or perhaps literally are not feasible.[3]

Closure has operated in the case of all three issues discussed in this chapter. In each case conditions have precluded alternatives, encouraging people to reject exclusionist ideology and adopt a no-fault strategy. With each of the three issues, I will consider the circumstances that close out alternatives to a no-fault course of action.

### THE WOMEN'S MOVEMENT AND THE NO-FAULT STRATEGY

I will begin with the women's movement. Since the mid–1800s American women have organized against male domination. Many early advocates of women's rights believed that women's subjugation would be largely overcome if they could obtain the vote. In Ida H. Harper's *The History of Woman Suffrage*, this ideological position was presented: "It was only a few of the clear thinkers, the far seeing, who realized at the beginning that the principal cause of women's inferior position and helplessness lay in their disenfranchisement and until they could be made to see it they were a dead weight on the movement."[4]

Events of the twentieth century indicate that the leaders of the voting-rights movement were wrong. Women received the vote, but the subjugation continued. The problem was that the source of women's predicament was much broader than simply their exclusion from the political structure.

In the late 1960s, the early leaders of the modern women's movement recognized that male domination permeated all structures of modern society. Kate Millett referred to the institutionalized "birthright priority" legitimating men's control of women. She wrote: "Through this system a most ingenious form of 'interior colonization' has been achieved. ...However muted its present appearance may be, sexual domination obtains nevertheless as perhaps the most pervasive ideology of our culture and provides its most fundamental concept of power."[5]

The modern women's movement has attacked sexism, the ideological position supporting male domination. Often the style has been direct and tough, certainly not what has traditionally been considered "lady-like." In the late 1960s and early 1970s, cover stories in *Time*, *Newsweek*, and other popular magazines presented an antiman, antifamily, bra-burning image of "women's lib." In spite of the negative publicity, the issue of women's rights quickly attracted widespread public support. As early as 1970, when the modern women's movement had barely appeared before the public eye, 42 percent of a national sample approved the efforts to strengthen or change women's status in society. It is hardly surprising that by 1981 when support for increased women's rights was no longer controversial, backing on this same issue had risen to 67 percent.[6]

More specifically Americans have shown an increasing willingness to support women's advancement in the economic area. In 1980, 32 percent of a national sample felt that the job opportunities for women had not gone far enough. Five years later, in spite of continuing improvement in this realm, the figure had risen to 41 percent.[7]

Married women have been one of the categories of women which has readily taken advantage of this improved climate of opinion. In fact, there has been a steady increase in the percentage of married women in the work force over the past quarter-century. In 1960, 28 percent of married women with the husband living in the home were in the labor force. By 1982 that figure had doubled, to 56 percent. The figures are even more dramatic for married women with the husband present and children under six years old. In 1960, 19 percent of this group were in the labor force; by 1982 the figure was more than two and a half times as great, or 49 percent.[8]

It should not be assumed that married women with children work simply for the money. A national survey conducted in 1985 found that when interviewers asked women to choose among a number of options involving marriage, children, and work the one judged most interesting and satisfying was marriage with children and a full-time job. Thirty-eight percent of women surveyed made this choice compared to 32 percent a decade earlier.[9]

Unfortunately choosing this option can create problems, even when women are successful at work. Such women often have found themselves wondering about the significance of their achievement. Many have not been able or willing to simply clone themselves in the narrow male hero-breadwinner image because they either already have husbands and children who represent a substantial portion of their personal commitment in life or because they want a family and appreciate the commitment that they must make to it. Here is where many modern women now stand—at what Betty Friedan has called "the second stage" of the modern women's movement. No longer is the struggle simply to wrest deserved rights from male-dominated structures. Now women who have achieved at least some of those rights wish to produce more order and happiness in their personal lives.

Several years ago Friedan went to a luncheon meeting of successful business and professional women. On this particular day, the women decided not to discuss how they would invest their money or seek to enter the "old boys' network" of real power. Instead they chose to examine the meaning of their success.

The vice-president of a large corporation explained that for seventeen years she had dedicated herself to her work. At first the only important concern had been to advance herself, but lately she had changed: "I hit some deep spiritual crisis or something. . . . I have to find the center of my own being." Just as she once realized that she was more than simply her husband's wife, she now was aware that she was more than a vice-president in the company: "I'm a person. Now I realize I've traded off too much for my career, traded off my family—too much." This woman decided that she had a serious problem soon after she had obtained significant power and influence in her company. "It's a real spiritual crisis when you reach that plateau and you realize . . . all those trimmings and trappings you'd been working for all those years, that's all there is."[10]

"That's all there is" is a plaintive conclusion. Because of increasingly available opportunities, this woman had a chance to develop occupational success, but she had largely pushed aside another set of needs—love and security, as embodied by marriage, children, home, and family.

How can one maximize both sets of needs? In her recent book, *The Second Stage*, Friedan has stressed that the modern women's movement needs to develop a new ideological position where cooperation, not conflict, between the sexes is emphasized. If wives, especially wives with young children, are going to develop careers, their husbands need to help at home. In the average-income American home, there is no alternative. Closure operates here.

A no-fault strategy on this issue opposes exclusionist ideology, asserting that the husband is no longer a hero. Instead he is an equal partner in what is becoming a two-person open covenant. Now the emphasis is on sharing rather than exclusionism. A marriage or a family becomes less a kingdom and more a community. Friedan and many others believe that the struggles of the "second stage" will continue for many years.

A recent study confirms this conclusion, indicating that even among married couples in which both are employed full-time and feel strongly that housework should be shared equally, women still tend to do considerably more.[11]

## THE ENVIRONMENTAL MOVEMENT AND THE NO-FAULT STRATEGY

For most of American history, the capitalist has had his way with the environment: He has been a single-minded exploiter. In William Dean Howells's novel *Silas Lapham*, one of Lapham's employees commented on his boss, a successful capitalist. "I think about the only difference between people in this world is that some know what they want, and some don't.... The old man knows what he wants every time. And generally he gets it."[12]

Nothing was permitted to stand in Lapham's way; he was driven by a dream for success and glory. For Lapham the holy quest was to sell as much of his paint as possible, preferably all around the world. For him paint was a passion. With his paint Lapham would leave his physical mark on the universe. He had made contacts in other countries, and it was his unshakeable belief that wherever a man had "a ship, or a bridge, or a dock, or a house, or a car, or a fence, or a pig-pen anywhere in God's universe to paint, that's the paint for him, and he's bound to find it out sooner or later."[13]

Driven by a passionate involvement in their enterprises, capitalists simply have done what needed to be done to expand their businesses and, like Lapham, leave their own physical mark on the earth. The different elements of the environment—timber, waterways, wildlife, air, soil, or whatever—were considered means to further their ambition and unimportant in themselves. Supported by the ideology of social Darwinism, they saw themselves as a superior group whose needs and interests were inextricably linked to national advancement.

The earliest organized effort to protect the environment was championed by a man of distinctly heroic qualities—President Theodore Roosevelt. As an outdoorsman and big game hunter, Roosevelt appreciated the natural resources of this country. Unlike most of his contemporaries, however, he also recognized their exhaustibility. Roosevelt was characteristically direct and firm in dealing with those whom he considered the major offenders—Western businessmen. In a speech in 1905, he explained that he hoped that men in the West would "remember the sharp distinction I have just drawn between the man who skins the land and the man who develops the country." Personally, Roosevelt explained, he would only work with the man who developed the country.[14]

Unfortunately Teddy Roosevelt was unusual. For the next three-quarters of a century, very few Americans were concerned about people "skinning" the land. Then in the 1960s, special circumstances produced a new ideological outlook on the environment.

Certainly one factor was Rachel Carson's *Silent Spring*. In 1962 she wrote this powerful, best-selling book, which opened with a description of a town in the heart of America where environmental harmony seemed to prevail. There were prosperous farms with fields of grain and hillsides of orchards. The surrounding woods were filled with oaks, maples, and birches, and the wildlife was abundant.

Then a strange blight moved into the area and everything started to change. Many of the cows, sheep, and chickens sickened and died. The farmers spoke of illness in their families, and doctors were puzzled by the new maladies. People wondered where the birds had gone. The feeding stations in the back yards were deserted, and the few birds that could still be seen trembled violently and could not fly. That spring the birds were silent. The once attractive roadsides now contained only browned and withered vegetation, which appeared to have been ravaged by fire. Even the fish had died.

In *Silent Spring* Rachel Carson stressed that by 1960 all these things had actually happened, though not in a single community. The source of the problems was the pesticide DDT, and her book was an assault on its indiscriminate use.[15] The book had a narrow focus and yet it has served as one of the opening sallies in the campaign launched by the environmental movement.

In 1969 a couple of events greatly increased public interest in and concern for the environment. At Santa Barbara, California, a massive oil spill, which coated the beaches and killed fish and fowl with its slime, received extensive press coverage. However, the issue that dominated public attention was something quite unexpected—the view from the moon of the fragile, finite "spaceship earth." No description or picture in the history of humanity has so graphically shown the state of vulnerability we earth dwellers share.

The poet Archibald MacLeish expressed feelings which many people had at the time: "To see the earth as it truly is, small and blue and beautiful in that eternal silence where it floats, is to see ourselves as riders on the earth together, brothers on that bright loveliness in the eternal cold—brothers who know now they are truly brothers."[16]

Our spaceship earth is small, blue, beautiful, and also fragile. To protect the earth, MacLeish suggested, we need to cooperate with each other. A world community of brothers and sisters would be compelled to work together to keep the fragile little ship on its course. Once again, it is suggested, problems (in this case environmental problems), will best be resolved with the acceptance of a no-fault strategy.

Recent survey data demonstrate a strong national concern for the environment. When asked whether they would make protection of the environment or economic growth a priority, 61 percent of a national sample in December 1984 chose environmental protection, even at the risk of curbing economic growth. Only 28 percent of the sample picked economic growth and 11 percent had another opinion or none at all. Those aged eighteen to forty-nine, the well-educated, and the more affluent were most inclined to support the environmental option.[17]

## THE ANTINUCLEAR MOVEMENT AND THE NO-FAULT STRATEGY

Like most modern nations, ours has a long list of military heroes: George Washington, John Paul Jones, Andrew Jackson, Ulysseus Grant, Theodore Roosevelt, John Pershing,

Dwight Eisenhower, and George Patton are prominent representatives.

Leaders and even common soldiers have been celebrated in history books, novels, films, television programs, and songs. However, they have become obsolete in modern warfare. During the Vietnam War, President Nixon withdrew all ground troops and concentrated on aerial bombardment. By the time that war was over, it seemed apparent that any future American war would be conducted with buttons, not soldiers, and would be brief.

Americans have been concerned about nuclear weaponry for decades. In October 1961 a small band of Americans and Europeans went to Moscow to seek Soviet cooperation in an effort to end nuclear buildup. In January 1962, 2,000 women picketed the White House in a heavy rainstorm, urging President Kennedy "to ban the bomb."[18]

Only in recent years, however, has an antinuclear ideology and a no-fault strategy received widespread support. One might wonder why. The most significant factor seems to have been Ronald Reagan's outlook on nuclear war. The Reagan team has indicated that relatively soon, perhaps by the end of this century, all the technological parts of a "winning" strategy could be in place—such innovations as antisatellite weapons and missile warheads with nearly perfect accuracy. The development of such technology promotes the idea that nuclear war "can be fought much like an old-fashioned artillery duel—limited, controlled, prolonged, with a winner and a loser."[19]

In deference to the Western image which Reagan covets, I would label his outlook on nuclear war "the shoot-out at the O.K. Corral" approach. In a situation where winning appears to be impossible, Reagan has at times declared that a winner definitely could emerge. Frequently, Reagan and his cohorts have been so taken with their image of American strength and destiny that they have written off the massive strength of the Soviet Union. Such a view is exlusionism at the extreme.

Perhaps, based on his activities in the early 1980s, Reagan should be awarded the Nobel Peace Prize. It seems that none of the opponents of nuclear escalation have had anything resembling his impact: He has scared the hell out of the American people and helped to educate them in the process. Consider the changing public reaction at the time Reagan was speaking bellicosely about the possibility of winning a nuclear war. In December 1982, 76 percent of a national sample indicated the belief that a nuclear war will spread once it starts. Exactly a year later, the figure had risen seven points to 83 percent. Over the same period of time, the percentage of informants who believed that both sides would be annihilated in a nuclear war increased from 73 to 83 percent.[20]

## THE TRAGIC NATURE OF THE NO-FAULT STRATEGY

Americans are starting to recognize that solutions to the three issues I have just considered require cooperation and a recognition of the equality of all participants. Right now it seems many people vaguely appreciate this necessity. The recognition, however, becomes much more compelling when individuals must face what William Lowrence has called "the tragic nature" of issues. The word "tragic" is not meant to suggest things that are "negative" or "terrible." Rather it refers to the necessity to understand "the way things are"— to look squarely at the truth and face the rock-bottom realities.[21] Nothing, it seems to me, produces an appreciation of the tragic nature of things quite the way personal action does, especially action which breaks down one's exclusionist habits and perceptions. Let us consider examples in the three areas.

A husband can talk endlessly about how important it is to support his wife's career by making a significant contribution to domestic tasks, but he undoubtedly will not have a tragic appreciation of domestic activity until he becomes involved in it.

For a year Mike McGrady, a journalist, maintained his home and cared for his three children while his wife went out to work. Almost immediately he began to learn the bitter realities about housework. For instance, there was the issue of keeping the home in order. At five o'clock one afternoon, McGrady returned from shopping to a house which he had cleaned up three hours earlier. The house was a mess, and McGrady told the children that it looked as if the place had been hit by a tornado. He asked them where their mother was. She'd come home, they explained, but when she saw the mess, she'd left. McGrady was worried; had their mother been angry? No, the children said, she laughed. McGrady explained that he wasn't laughing; he'd spent half the day cleaning up, and now they were going to have to restore order before their mother came home again.[22]

McGrady discovered how difficult, time-consuming, and unrewarding housework could be. He also learned that being a housewife or househusband could be demeaning. One problem lay in the need to take money from his wife. McGrady pointed out that in a long-term marriage like his, the spouses are bound by many elements. He wrote: "This ritual, the giving of allowance by one human being to another, bespeaks whole planets of meaning; it has to do with independence, gratification, reward, punishment, resentment."[23] The feelings are so complicated, McGrady suggested, that he doubted they could be understood by men until like him they switched roles and became recipients instead of donors. McGrady never found it easy to take money from his wife. From the first week to the last, he tried to minimize the transaction by grabbing his wife's check and cramming it into his wallet as quickly as possible. For McGrady, taking money from his wife was the essence of the tragic issue. Any abstraction about switching roles was obliberated when she handed him the check.

Facing the tragic nature of the environmental issue is not easily accomplished either. For Lois Gibbs, however, it has been a more obvious step to take than for most Americans. Gibbs was a resident of Love Canal, a section of which was heavily polluted by an enormous local deposit of chemical wastes. In August 1978 Robert Whalen, the New York state health commissioner, spoke to the local residents, summarizing expert opinion about the extent of danger. To many listeners, including Gibbs, his speech was a clear understatement of the dangers. Eventually Gibbs became so angry and frustrated that she stood up and shouted, "You're murdering us!" That statement represented Gibbs's first public revelation of her confrontation with the tragic nature of the environmental crisis in her own community. Soon Lois Gibbs became well known, not only in western New York state but throughout the country.[24]

Several months before making the statement, Lois Gibbs became convinced that the locally high rates of miscarriage, birth defects, and other illnesses and disabilities were linked to the chemical wastes that had been buried in the earth several decades earlier. However, she did not know what to do. She was particularly concerned about the school her son was attending. Someone told her that if she really wanted action, she should get ten mothers to picket the school for ten days, and then it certainly would be closed down.

Gibbs was frightened at the thought of such a bold action; yet she was convinced that something had to be done. Eventually she decided that the best thing was to form a parents' group that would demand the cleanup of the school area so that it would be absolutely safe. On the first day of this new endeavor, Gibbs forced herself to walk to a house near the school. She knocked on the door. "To her great relief, no one answered. 'I ran home, thinking, "well I tried!' " She stayed home for a full day, but once the initial feelings of relief had subsided, she realized that she must keep trying, even though she was 'scared stiff at the thought.' "[25] Lois Gibbs had started to face the tragic nature of the local pollution issue. She was convinced that something had to be done, or the illnesses would continue. Certainly no heroes would lead the way.

Gradually Gibbs became more and more effective at presenting the citizens' case. She had a lot of help, including that of her brother-in-law, a biologist with a keen interest in environmental issues. One thing he taught her was how to deal with the media. The first time Lois encountered the media she spoke emotionally and impulsively. Afterwards her brother-in-law advised her to have a good set of questions ready for any meeting where the media were present and to make sure to ask the questions within the first fifteen minutes because after that media people usually left to file their reports.[26]

Eventually Lois Gibbs and other local citizens formed the Love Canal Homeowners Association, and after two years of battling the state and federal governments, a period of time in which many frustrations and set-backs occurred, they won. A complex agreement was reached whereby federal and state officials agreed to purchase the homes of all Love Canal residents living in the endangered area.

At that time a journalist asked Gibbs whether she believed that this outcome showed "that 'the little guy' could finally win against 'the big guys.' Gibbs replied: 'No, that's wrong. We're not little people! We're the big people who vote them in. We have the power; they don't.' "[27] This was a very different Lois Gibbs from the shy woman who two years earlier had been relieved to find that no one was home in the house near her son's school. She had looked hard at the tragic nature of the local environmental crisis and then firmly, if at first tremulously, had taken steps to change it.

Perhaps facing the tragic nature of the issue is even more difficult where nuclear weaponry is concerned. As one writer pointed out, MX sounds like it should be a sports car and MIRVs (multiple independently targetable reentry vehicles) sound like a new Atari game. Then this writer added, "Since these devices can turn flesh to molten paste in seconds, the use of high-tech lingo for talking about Armageddon is no accident."[28]

In recent years many antinuclear protesters have become aware of the problem of breaking down this abstraction and compelling people to face the tragic nature of the nuclear issue. To make the issue seem more real, some activists have dumped or smeared their own blood at protest sites. In many cases reporters, police officers, lawyers, and judges are almost unable to utter the single word "blood" when it is spilled at these sites. Instead they'll speak of red paint, red dye, "a red substance," animal blood, or "what they said was their own blood."

The Reverend William J. Snyder, an activist with one peace group, explained that it is relatively easy to discuss the production of nuclear weapons and the arms race in abstract terms. As long as the discussion remains abstract, it is possible to debate whether the death of 140 million people is an acceptable loss in a preemptive strike. At that point it is like playing a giant war game, but the situation changes as soon as blood enters the picture. Blood eliminates abstraction. All of us have seen blood coming from people we love. We have struggled with handkerchiefs and bandages to stem the flow of blood from our children's gashes and nosebleeds. Referring to a particular protest, Snyder concluded that the protesters were suggesting that discussions about the acceptable risk of 140 million deaths "is really about 140 million nosebleeds and gashes which can't be healed. This is why they poured a certain 'red substance' inside General Electric."[29]

## CONCLUSION

It was very difficult for Lois Gibbs to knock on that first door. Nothing terrible could have happened. Nevertheless, she may not have been consciously aware at that moment that she was not facing imminent doom. Most of us spend our entire lives doing only things that are acceptable to others. We live within the standard covenants. Lois was frightened because, alone and by herself, she was taking a step into the unknown where the values and standards were not mapped out. She took the step and found herself unhurt, still breathing regularly and, if anything, feeling more alive than before. Those who poured blood at protest sites took the same step. It is very possible that in the spirit of the open covenant, many more, each in his or her own chosen way, will take a similar step in the years ahead.

## SUMMARY

This chapter has examined the no-fault strategy, which is perhaps the most promising step toward the realization of the open covenant. I discussed the two basic qualities found in that particular course of action—cooperation and equality of participants. Then I considered how closure has operated to make the no-fault strategy applicable to three modern social movements—the "second stage" of the modern women's movement, the environmental movement, and the antinuclear movement. Finally there was a discussion offering illustrations of how people face the tragic nature of issues that are central to these three social movements—housework, environmental pollution, and the prospect of nuclear war.

# 9

## The Open Covenant

Every child knows the story of "The Sleeping Beauty," but perhaps it is forgotten later on. The story tells how in a particular kingdom, a king and queen had a beautiful daughter. She was so beautiful that as she grew up, the king could not contain himself with joy, and so he ordered a great feast. Among those who were invited were all the known wise women in the kingdom. Actually only twelve of the thirteen wise women were invited, because there were only twelve golden plates from which they could eat. It has always seemed to me that this was asking for trouble, but no matter. At any rate, during the feast the wise women gave the young girl precious gifts—virtue, beauty, riches, and other things. Then, suddenly, the uninvited wise woman appeared. Burning with revenge she explained that she also had a gift to give. When the princess reached fifteen years of age, the woman said, she would prick her finger with a spindle and fall dead. After describing her "gift," the unwanted guest left.

Everyone was stunned. Then the last of the wise women came forward: She had not yet bestowed her gift. This woman explained that while she lacked the power to do away with the evil prophecy, she could soften its impact. She said, "The princess shall not die, but fall into a deep sleep for a hundred years." That, in fact, is what happened. When the princess pricked her finger, all living creatures, human and otherwise, fell asleep in the castle. Then, a century later, a young prince arrived, kissed the princess, and the two lived happily ever after to the end of their days.[1]

There is one point I find particularly provocative about this story: I mean the part about the twelfth wise woman, the one who waited to give her gift until the very end. The critical thing is that while she could not undo the evil that had been done, she could lessen its impact considerably. While this wise woman was superhuman, she was not all-powerful. In her wisdom she looked hard and clearly at the tragic nature of the issue before her and prescribed the best solution available. I find her an inspiring model because, it seems to me, this is the same course of action that we need to follow with our most troubling social issues today. Realistically we can not deny the existence of the issues. They exist, but if we use wisdom we can deal with them effectively.

As we saw in the last chapter, some Americans have started to confront these critical social issues. Nevertheless, there remains a long way to go. "Why bother?" one might ask. We bother because we fervently want to preserve and nurture life. We want our biological children as well as our children in spirit to grow up and thrive in a better world. If those of us who care do nothing—if we let our world be controlled by those whose priorities are money and power—then, probably, our planet will be destroyed.

"All right," the questioner continues. "I can buy that, but I have got a tougher question. How do we get anything meaningful done? We're all so puny as individuals. I feel so damned powerless." Undoubtedly at times everyone does, but there are steps that can be taken.

## LAUNCHING THE OPEN COVENANT

During the 1950s Muzafer Sherif conducted a series of psychological experiments on young boys at a summer camp. Sherif divided twelve-year-olds into two groups of a dozen each and gave each group real-life problems that could only be resolved by working together. As the members of each group worked together and resolved their problems, they became increasingly fond of each other. Once these tasks were completed, Sherif initiated a series of competitive contests, where each individual member of the group who won received a highly prized four-blade jackknife. As the competition intensified, the members of each group started making nasty comments about the other, and raids on each other's cabins became commonplace. When the hostility was at its peak, Sherif tried to unite the two groups by suggesting that the members of both groups had a common enemy, a group of threatening outsiders. This strategy produced some success, but the boys within each group still maintained hostile feelings toward each other.

The following year Sherif experimented with another set of boys and followed the same steps to produce intergroup hostility. This time, however, he sought other ways of reducing the hostility. First, he brought the two groups into a pleasant, noncompetitive atmosphere, where they ate excellent food together and watched movies. This effort was unsuccessful; the boys shouted at each other and some started to fight.

Then Sherif tried another strategy. He confronted the hostile groups with problems that only could be resolved if they cooperated with each other. In one instance the camp water supply stopped, and the boys had to work together to find the leak in a mile-long pipe. In another situation the truck used to bring food would not start, and both groups had to pull together, using a tug-of-war rope, to get the truck started. These superordinate goals, which could only be achieved by intergroup cooperation, did not produce immediate positive intergroup feelings but eventually caused relations between members of the two groups to improve. When hostilities were at their peak, none of the boys had friendships outside their own groups, while after the cooperative activities 30 percent of friendships were intergroup. Furthermore, following cooperation, group members' negative feelings for boys outside their own group sharply declined.[2]

Essentially this analysis reframes in an abbreviated form the issues discussed at length in chapter 8. Superordinate goals often employ the no-fault strategy. Instead of focusing on their differences and hostilities, Sherif's second group of boys was encouraged to overcome their differences and work as equals to achieve mutually satisfying goals. Those promoting the second stage of the women's movement, the environmental movement, and the antinuclear movement are doing much the same thing.

Superordinate goals could be established for the entire planet. At the conclusion of *War*, Gwynne Dyer proposed that the best way to eliminate war and, above all, to prevent nuclear war, is to remove the structures in whose interest those wars are started—national states. Dyer realized that such a plan would not mean that people

> will end up loving one another indiscriminately, but that isn't necessary. There is not universal love and brotherhood *within* national states either. What does exist, and what must now be extended beyond national borders, is a mutual recognition that everybody is better off if they respect each other's rights and accept arbitration by a higher authority rather than shooting each other when their rights come into conflict.[3]

The launching of the open covenant requires a new set of superordinate goals such as those expressed above and in the previous chapter. There must also be a willingness to take chances by stepping outside the standard way of doing things. Let me give a couple of examples.

David Cooper was teaching English at the University of California at Santa Barbara. One day, a few hours before class, he decided to discuss nuclear weaponry and protests against it. At colleges and universities, academic freedom has assured teachers a leeway that employees generally lack in the commercial world, so it was no problem to run off copies of several articles for his students. It was also easy to present the nuclear issue for discussion and writing in the classroom. Cooper wrote: "Those words we had used to help us explore literature—aggression, hostility, deception, endurance, human triumph—could easily be borrowed to help us see the relationship between nuclear weapons and cultural suicide."[4]

The students' reaction surprised Cooper. He had always suspected that it was hopeless to try to convince students to become really interested in big issues, but instead they were deeply interested. There was a strange twist, however. They were excited and simultaneously afraid, not afraid of confronting the nightmarish nuclear issue but afraid that their writing skills weren't up to the task.

A senior visited Cooper one day during his office hours. He explained that he had read the two papers which had been assigned and that he agreed with their content. There was a problem, however. The assignment asked that he provide "a student perspective" on the nuclear issue, and this senior felt he lacked the background to attack such a task. Obviously embarrassed he said, "I've never been asked to consider this issue before." Cooper wrote, "Four years at the university and the obvious concern and sensitivity that was there had not been drawn out into the open."[5]

Cooper was impressed by two themes in the students' presentations. First, they were very critical of themselves and their peers because of their apathy about the nuclear issue. They readily admitted that they had not even remotely come to grips with the issue—that their overall sense of security only dealt with financial and professional success and did not even address the spectre of nuclear war. Second, and more significant, the students felt that the university had failed them profoundly. Many students would have liked to have been offered a set of courses on peace studies and, in particular, an interdisciplinary course on arms control and nuclear war. Recruits for the courses would have been no problem; Cooper was convinced that forty students would have signed up instantly from his class alone.

It seems to me that David Cooper hit on several important points. It is very likely that teachers are in the best position to raise the kinds of prominent social problems discussed in this book. As Cooper noted, they are freer than people in most other positions. Furthermore their mandate is to educate young people, and a critical part of education is to encourage students to come to grips with the compelling issues of our time.

As David Cooper discovered, just starting a dialogue is a meaningful step. Recently I attended a meeting at Southern

Connecticut State University where the speakers were two members of the Soviet mission to the United Nations. For many present it was their first contact with live Soviet citizens. It was readily apparent that they had neither horns nor scaly skin. They looked like businessmen or academics, and they discussed a variety of topics and answered questions calmly, self-assuredly, and firmly. Toward the end of the session, a student asked "whether you guys have plans to get out of Afghanistan." People laughed; Americans have called Soviet citizens many things, but "you guys" was new. Nevertheless, the term appeared consistent with the way in which many at the meeting seemed to be feeling. Certainly, the Soviet representatives were from the other side, but they were seen as opponents, not enemies. While the meeting obviously did not resolve international differences, it was an evening well spent. Some barriers were broken down: It was a small part of a struggle that must continue.

The situations described above involve actions that support the development of the open covenant. However, their significance is small, even miniscule, and they have had little or no long-term impact. For the development of the open covenant to occur, structures and values must change. I can think of only one primary place where such change is likely to be initiated—in schools.

## EDUCATION AND THE OPEN COVENANT

At the moment I feel a bit like the football coach who looks nervously at his bench during a losing contest and sees just one scrawny substitute who might possibly save the game. Certainly education is not celebrated for its current accomplishments. It is widely believed that educational reform in the 1960s and 1970s helped undermine standards of learning and that what this system needs is renewed discipline and a reestablishment of traditional standards. What educators often view as current student deficiencies—a refusal to become excited or to do more than the minimum—are often blamed on the education system. My suspicion is that hopelessness, fear, and confusion associated with job prospects and such threats as environmental destruction and nuclear war are as much the sources of such reactions as are deficiencies in the schools.

I believe that the scrawny substitute on the bench might surprise many of us. Let us consider some of the issues involving the open covenant that could be confronted in schools. Each issue which is raised will involve a central theme of the earlier chapters.

As we saw in chapters 2 and 3, the Puritan legacy still maintains a stronghold in our society. While most modern Americans no longer strive for salvation in the next world, we do seem to be seeking it now. Individual pursuits and group cooperation are not highly compatible. Educators supporting the open covenant need to confront this issue in the schools, and the topic could be initiated with young children.

I don't think that this is a simple issue. It would be foolhardy to expect Americans to simply eliminate all individual goals and strivings. After all, our economic and cultural systems are primarily individualistic. The challenge, it appears, is to begin to develop and use new systems that are less militantly competitive and that encourage and reward group more than individualistic outcomes. It will be interesting to see where educators could obtain support for such approaches outside the schools.

In chapter 3 heroes and presidents as heroes comprised an important theme. In schools a number of individuals, including some presidents, are glorified as heroes, but they are seldom analyzed. Infrequently is it suggested that they might be an ambivalent or even negative force in Americans' lives.

It seems to me that the subject of heroes could provide material for an interesting course at the high-school or college level. Topics to cover would include:

The definition of the hero;

The analysis of heroes in other cultures;

The examination of heroes in American culture;

Women as heroes; and

The hero in the future.

The last topic, in particular, might include an examination of the distinction between heroes and role models. As we grow up, most of us probably find it useful and sometimes even inspiring to observe and emulate individuals who successfully accomplish the tasks we would like to perform. Unlike heroes, however, such people do not receive our unquestioning allegiance in exchange for their support and comfort. Role models simply provide general guidance and direction.

In chapter 4 we observed that many modern families are locked into some intermediate point between traditionalism and modernity, which is probably located closer to the former. While both high schools and colleges offer courses on the family, there might be increased emphasis on the topics of communication and bargaining. If the couple relationship is to be visualized as a two-person open covenant, what skills must people learn so that they can maximize their individual and collective goals and insure or at least improve the possibility of cooperation? The couple relationship seems to be a lucrative situation for developing the skills of the open covenant. People who can communicate and bargain actively and compassionately with their mates will probably develop skills that can be used in other areas. In addition, they will be prime candidates for a strong, enduring marriage which, in itself, is an accomplishment these days.

The schools are the key to progress toward the open covenant, and it is my hope that in the years ahead there will be many long, vocal, and provocative discussions (and even arguments) about curriculum development. Earlier I suggested that while educational reforms in the 1960s and early 1970s were relatively unsuccessful, in part because of a deemphasis on scholastic standards and discipline, the philosophy behind them makes a great deal of sense in the present context. If people are going to learn to appreciate the need and develop the capacity to cooperate on various controversial issues, the schools need to contribute citizens who are imaginative, creative, and excited by the prospect of a more peaceful, equitable world.

Were I in a position to formulate national policy in education, I would put a strong emphasis on making school fun, exciting, and creative. These are the things I would do differently. First, I would spend a great deal more money on teacher salaries, encouraging a greater number of vibrant young people to enter the field. Second, I would try to establish new policies that would enlarge the relationship between the classroom and the outside world, realizing that people can only realistically work for something better when they more completely understand the qualities of what they already have. The procedure would involve bringing a rich variety of individuals and groups into schools as well as taking children from school to many outside agencies and organizations. Moreover, I am not referring to occasional class trips or exercises. Fairly young students, for instance, might be apprenticed for a week, a month, or even a year to some business or activity so that they could be in a position to learn about it in depth.

In conclusion, were I in charge of educational policy, my mission would be two-fold: first, to abolish the dullness in the eyes, the monotony in the voices, and the grayness in the spirits of today's students; and, second, to develop the understanding and skills that will help realize the open covenant.

Now I will confront a particularly difficult issue. As I indicated in Chapter 6, bureaucracies and work organizations in general are strongly disinclined to change. They have their distinct goals and procedures, and these tend to be exclusionist, opposing the development of the open covenant. While business organizations and educational systems can work together, the most pronounced evidence of such a relationship in recent years has been the development of business programs in colleges and universities to service the sharply increased proportion of students who want to enter the business world.

As far as the goal of an open covenant is concerned, the relationship between schools and work bureaucracies would be a very different one. Students might study the various ways they could support mutual understanding and cooperation within a bureacracy or even between different organizations. They might consider the fact that there is a variety of viewpoints people might maintain toward doing their jobs, and analyze the likely rewards and punishments for failing to obey different organizational regulations. The work world and its demands constitute a difficult subject for those supporting the open covenant, and yet some interesting issues and projects related to the topic could be explored in school.

At the present moment, in the decade of the eighties, the topic of the "slow thaw" is not particularly popular. On the surface this appears to be a very conservative era, a throwback in certain respects to the 1950s. Toward the end of chapter 7, however, we saw that this analysis is a distinct simplification. To most readers that information was probably new and perhaps surprising. My conviction is that most of us know very little about changes in American values over time.

There is fertile material in this area for educational programs. Most students probably do not know what values and ideologies are, and they certainly have little concrete sense of how they influence us. Teachers of history and sociology could work cooperatively here, developing courses and programs about changing world and American values over time. A high-school course which requires students to study contemporary values, determining their sources and impacts and discussing and debating students' own values could be fascinating. At the end of such a course, the students might construct a set of values they would choose as guidelines for the future. The open covenant would probably not fare very well in many classrooms. From my perception the open covenant's evaluation is much less important than encouraging students to confront the issues with which the ideology of the open covenant is concerned.

The three topics related to the no-fault strategy and discussed in chapter 8 are well-known modern issues, and they are all discussed in schools and in texts, particularly the gender-role issue. However, as David Cooper's venture into a discussion of the nuclear topic demonstrated, this issue receives little thorough examination. My impression is that even in courses where the nuclear and environmental issues are examined, the treatment is more likely to be at the technical than at the cultural level. Even the subject of gender-role could be analyzed in new and different ways. I suspect, for instance, that people who support the second stage of the modern women's movement in their daily lives would be more inclined than nonsupporters of the second stage to involve themselves in the antinuclear and environmental movements: Students could research this issue. In the course of such activity, they would invariably develop a more detailed understanding about topics related to the open covenant.

## CONCLUSION

Not long ago someone suggested to me that the problem with the quest for peace is that it doesn't excite people. In an age where stimulation and titillation are at a premium peace just doesn't score well.

Certainly the person who suggested this hypothesis is right as far as salient values are concerned. Most young people, and many who are older as well, will find it a great deal more stimulating to see Rambo killing a group of communists than to sit around and discuss the prospects of lasting world peace. Admittedly the Rambo types currently have the inside track on raw excitement.

For a moment, however, let's do something that people today are seldom encouraged to do. Let's be willing to admit that, individually and collectively, many of us have made significant mistakes. Instead of the way we live, let's think about leading lives that possess consistency, continuity, and sanity. How many of us can truly make the claim that our lives represent a clear contribution to the current welfare and the continuing survival of humanity? Not many, I suspect. Wouldn't it be profoundly exciting to be able to make such a claim?

Perhaps a final little story can help convey that spirit. This one concerns a traveller's observations about the difference between heaven and hell. On the first leg of his trip, the traveller accompanied by a guide went to hell where he saw people walking around with long wooden spoons as arms. Feeding themselves was quite futile, because they could not put the food directly into their mouths; usually they would throw it in the air and it would fall on the floor. Afterwards the traveller moved on to heaven. Soon after arriving he turned to his guide and explained with some irritation—after all, it had been a long trip—that since the people here too had wooden spoons for arms, he really could not see any difference between heaven and hell. However then they brought out food, and the traveller saw that there was a profound difference: In heaven the people fed each other.

## SUMMARY

Launching the open covenant involves concrete efforts by dedicated individuals and groups. I discussed this issue at a general level, introducing the concept of superordinate goals. I also examined the topic at a concrete level, looking at David Cooper's revealing efforts to encourage students to confront their feelings about the possibility of nuclear war. This chapter also considered how some of the issues related to the open covenant and analyzed in earlier chapters could be effectively confronted in schools.

# Notes

## Chapter 1

1. Aldous Huxley, *Brave New World* (New York: Bantam Books, 1946), 12–14.
2. Karl Mannheim, *Ideology and Utopia* (New York: Harcourt, Brace & World, 1936), 59–75.
3. Daniel Bell, *The End of Ideology* (Glencoe, Ill.: Free Press, 1960).
4. Stephen W. Rousseas and James Farganis, "American Politics and the End of Ideology," in *The New Sociology*, ed. Irving Louis Horowitz (New York: Oxford University Press, 1964), 284.
5. Theodore Roszak, *The Making of a Counter Culture* (Garden City, N.Y.: Anchor Books, 1969), 10–11.

## Chapter 2

1. Kenneth Lockridge, *A New England Town: The First Hundred Years* (New York: W. W. Norton & Company, 1970), 4.
2. Ibid., 4–7.
3. Ibid., 80–85.
4. Robert Pope, *The Half-Way Convenant: Church Membership in Puritan New England* (Princeton: Princeton University Press, 1969), 274.
5. Ibid., 169.

## Chapter 3

1. Bronislaw Malinowski, *Magic, Science, and Religion and Other Essays* (Garden City, N.Y.: Doubleday and Company, 1948), 30.

2. Max Weber, *The Protestant Ethic and the Spirit of Capitalism*, trans. Talcott Parsons (New York: Charles Scribner's Sons, 1948), 103–4.

3. Ibid., 109.

4. Ibid., 51–52.

5. Richard Hofstadter, *Social Darwinism in American Thought*, rev. ed. (Boston: Beacon Press, 1955), 45.

6. Robin Williams, Jr., *American Society*, 3rd ed. (New York: Alfred A. Knopf, 1970), 454.

7. Robert Merton, *Social Theory and Social Structure*, rev. ed. (Glencoe, Ill.: Free Press, 1957), 142.

8. Williams, *American Society*, 458.

9. Ibid., 460–61.

10. Jeanne Humphrey Block, "Conceptions of Sex Role: Some Cross-Cultural and Longitudinal Perspectives," *American Psychologist* 28 (June 1973): 512–26.

11. Marshall Fishwick, *The Hero, American Style* (New York: David McKay Company, 1969).

12. George Vecsey, "The Other Side," *New York Times*, 14 July 1985, sec. 5, p. 3.

13. Kevin P. Phillips, *Post-Conservative America: People, Politics, and Ideology in a Time of Crisis* (New York: Vintage Books, 1983), 155–64.

14. Max Weber, *From Max Weber: Essays in Sociology*, trans. and ed. H. H. Gerth and C. Wright Mills (New York: Oxford University Press, 1946), 245–48.

15. Steven R. Weisman, "The Politics of Popularity," *New York Times*, 8 November 1984, sec. A, p. 19.

16. Jeff Meer, "Reagan's Facial Teflon," *Psychology Today* 20 (January 1986): 18.

17. Lance Morrow, "Yankee Doodle Magic," *Time* 128, (7 July 1986): 14.

18. *CBS News Poll*, 6 March 1987; *Washington Post–ABC News Poll*, June 1987.

19. Bernard Bailyn et al. *The Great Republic* (Lexington, Mass: D. C. Heath and Company, 1977), 1185.

20. George Gallup, Jr., *Gallup Poll*, November/December 1984.

## Chapter 4

1. Jerome Kagan, "The Psychological Requirements for Human Development," in *Family in Transition*, ed. Arlene S. Skolnick and

Jerome H. Skolnick, 4th ed. (Boston: Little, Brown and Company, 1983), 409–20.

2. William J. Goode, *World Revolution and Family Patterns* (New York: Free Press, 1963).

3. Christopher Lasch, "The Family as a Haven in a Heartless World." in *Family in Transition*, ed. Arlene S. Skolnick and Jerome H. Skolnick, 3rd ed. (Boston: Little, Brown and Company, 1980), 80–91.

4. Betty Friedan, *The Feminine Mystique* (New York: W. W. Norton and Company, 1963).

5. Richard Sennett, *Families against the City* (New York: Vintage Books, 1974).

6. William Goode, *The Family*, 2nd ed. (Englewood Cliffs, N.J.: Prentice-Hall, 1982), 89–90.

7. Philip E. Slater, *The Pursuit of Loneliness* (Boston: Beacon Press, 1971), 59.

8. U.S. Bureau of the Census, *Statistical Abstract of the United States: 1986*, 106th ed. no. 81 (Washington, D.C.: U.S. Government Printing Office, 1986).

9. Phillipe Ariès, "The Family, Prison of Love," *Psychology Today* 9 (August 1975): 53–58.

10. Philip Blumstein and Pepper Schwartz, *American Couples* (New York: William Morrow and Company, 1983), 319–22.

11. Paul C. Glick, "How American Families Are Changing," in *Marriage and Family: 85/86* (Guilford, Conn.: Dushkin Publishing Group, 1985), 21–24.

12. Peter J. Stein, "Singlehood: An Alternative to Marriage," in *Family in Transition*, ed. Arlene S. Skolnick and Jerome H. Skolnick, 3rd ed. (Boston: Little, Brown and Company, 1980), 517.

## Chapter 5

1. Peter Binzen, *Whitetown USA* (New York: Random House, 1970), 41–42.

2. Quoted in Binzen, *Whitetown USA*, 42–43.

3. Ibid., 43.

4. Philip Jackson, *Life in Classrooms* (New York: Holt, Rinehart and Winston, 1968), 6.

5. Harry L. Gracey, "Learning the Student Role: Kindergarten as Academic Boot Camp," in *Readings in Introductory Sociology*, ed. Dennis H. Wrong and Harry L. Gracey, 3rd ed. (New York: Macmillan, 1977), 215–26.

6. Charles A. Reich, *The Greening of America* (New York: Bantam Books, 1971), 148.

7. J. W. Getzels and P. W. Jackson, "Occupational Choice and Cognitive Functioning," *Journal of Abnormal and Social Psychology* (February 1960), reported in *Schooling in Capitalist America: Educational Reform and the Contradictions of Economic Life*, ed. Samuel Bowles and Herbert Gintis (New York: Basic Books, 1976), 40.

8. James Herndon, *How to Survive in Your Native Land* (New York: Bantam Books, 1972), 24–25.

9. Ibid., 27.

10. Milton Goldberg and James Harvey, "A Nation at Risk: The Report of the National Commission on Excellence in Education," *Phi Delta Kappan* 65 (September 1983): 14–18.

11. Pamela Bardo, "The Pain of Teacher Burnout: A Case History," *Phi Delta Kappan* 61 (December 1979): 252.

12. George Gallup, Jr., *Gallup Poll*, September 1986.

## Chapter 6

1. Max Weber, *From Max Weber: Essays in Sociology*, 196–98.

2. Arthur Miller, "The Crucible," in *Arthur Miller's Collected Plays* (New York: Viking Press, 1957), 228.

3. Robert K. Merton, *Social Theory and Social Structure*, 3rd ed. (New York: The Free Press, 1968), 177–78.

4. William H. Whyte, Jr., *The Organization Man* (New York: Simon and Schuster, 1956), 33.

5. Ibid., 52.

6. Irving L. Janis, *Victims of Groupthink: A Psychological Study of Foreign-Policy Decisions and Fiascoes* (Boston: Houghton Mifflin Company, 1972), 42.

7. Lindsey Gruson, "Philadelphia Should Have Taken Early Assault Advice, Panel Told," *New York Times*, 23 October 1985, p. 16.

8. Christopher Bates Doob, *How the War Was Lost: A Description and Analysis of Anti-Poverty Groups in Two Areas* (Unpublished manuscript), 43.

9. Ibid., 83.

10. Ibid., 91.

11. Gideon Sjoberg, Ted. S. Vaughan, and Norma Williams, "Bureaucracy as a Moral Issue," *Journal of Applied Behavioral Science* 20 (1984): 441–53.

## Chapter 7

1. Robin Williams, Jr., *American Society*, 462–64.

2. Ibid., 473.

3. Mark Twain, "The Anglo-Saxon Race," in *Mark Twain and the Three R's*, ed. Maxwell Geismar (Indianapolis: Bobbs-Merrill Company, 1973), 3.

4. Jack Kerouac, *On the Road* (New York: Viking Press, 1957), 105.

5. Ibid., 19.

6. Ibid., 33.

7. Ibid., 180.

8. George Gallup, Jr., *Gallup Poll*, March 1969.

9. George Gallup, Jr., *Gallup Poll*, May 1971.

10. J. Anthony Lukas, *Don't Shoot—We Are Your Children* (New York: Random House, 1971), 160.

11. Robert M. Pirsig, *Zen and the Art of Motorcycle Maintenance* (New York: William Morrow and Company, 1974), 218.

12. Ibid., 218.

13. George Gallup, Jr., *Gallup Poll*, May 1985.

14. Daniel Yankelovich, *New Rules: Searching for Self-Fulfillment in a World Turned Upside Down* (New York: Random House, 1981), 251.

15. Karlyn Keene and Daniel Yankelovich, "American Values: Change and Stability," *Public Opinion* 6 (January 1984): 2–8, 21–35; National Opinion Research Center, combined survey results from 1983–1986.

## Chapter 8

1. J. R. R. Tolkien, *The Fellowship of the Ring*, part I of *The Lord of the Rings*, 2nd ed. (Boston: Houghton Mifflin, 1965), 362.

2. Lenore J. Weitzman and Ruth B. Dixon, "The Transformation of Marriage through No-Fault Divorce," in *Family in Transition*, ed. Arlene S. Skolnick and Jerome H. Skolnick, 4th ed. (Boston: Little, Brown and Company, 1983), 353–66.

3. Edwin M. Lemert, "An Isolation and Closure Theory of Naive Check Forgery," in *Human Deviance, Social Problems, and Social Control*, ed. Edwin M. Lemert, 2nd ed. (Englewood Cliffs, N.J.: Prentice-Hall, 1972), 137–49.

4. Ida Husted Harper, ed., *The History of Woman Suffrage*, vol. 5

(New York: National American Woman Suffrage Association, 1922), xv.

5. Kate Millett, *Sexual Politics* (Garden City, N.Y.: Doubleday and Company, 1970), 25.

6. Louis Harris, *Harris Survey*, August 1981.

7. Burns Roper, *Roper Reports*, February 1985.

8. U. S. Department of Labor, *The Female-Male Earning Gap: A Review of Employment and Earnings Issues* (September 1982), table 2.

9. George Gallup, Jr., *Gallup Poll*, May 1985.

10. Betty Friedan, *The Second Stage* (New York: Summit Books, 1981), 62.

11. Blumstein and Schwartz, *American Couples*, p. 145.

12. William Dean Howells, *The Rise of Silas Lapham* (Boston: Houghton Mifflin Company, 1912), 146.

13. Ibid., 22.

14. Theodore Roosevelt, *American Problems*, vol. 16 in *The Works of Theodore Roosevelt* (New York: Charles Scribner's Sons, 1926), 106.

15. Rachel Carson, *Silent Spring* (Boston: Houghton Mifflin Company, 1962).

16. Archibald MacLeish, "Brothers in the Eternal Cold," *Reader's Digest* 94 (March 1969): 68–69.

17. George Gallup, Jr., *Gallup Poll*, December 1984.

18. *Newsweek*, "Picketing the President," 59 (29 January 1962): 19; *Time*, "March to Moscow," 78 (13 October 1961): 32.

19. Leslie H. Gelb, "Is the Nuclear Threat Manageable?" *New York Times Magazine*, 4 March 1984, p. 29.

20. Burns Roper, *Roper Reports*, December 1983.

21. William W. Lowrance, "The Agenda for Risk Decisionmaking," *Environment* 25 (December 1983): 4–8.

22. Mike McGrady, *The Kitchen Sink Papers* (Garden City, N.Y.: Doubleday and Company, 1975), 47–49.

23. Ibid., 27.

24. Adeline Gordon Levine, *Love Canal: Science, Politics, and People* (Lexington, Mass.: Lexington Books, 1982), 27–29.

25. Ibid., 31.

26. Ibid., 32.

27. Ibid., 208–209.

28. Caryl Rivers, "Armageddon Lingo," *New York Times*, 2 February 1984, p. 19.

29. Samuel H. Day, Jr., "The New Resistance," *Progressive* (April 1983): 27.

## Chapter 9

1. Jacob and Wilhelm Grimm, *Household Stories*, trans. Lucy Crane (New York: Dover Publications, 1963), 204–7.

2. Muzafer Sherif, *Social Interaction: Processes and Products* (Chicago: Aldine, 1967).

3. Gwynne Dyer, *War* (New York: Crown Publishers, 1985), 264.

4. David Cooper, "When Students Tried to Think about the Nuclear Arms Race," *Center Magazine* 15 (July/August 1982): 4.

5. Ibid., 4.

# Selected Bibliography

Ariès, Phillipe. "The Family, Prison of Love." *Psychology Today* 9 (August 1975): 53–58.

Bell, Daniel. *The End of Ideology*. Glencoe, Ill.: Free Press, 1960.

Berger, Brigitte, and Peter L. Berger. *The War over the Family: Capturing the Middle Ground*. Garden City, N.Y.: Anchor Books, 1984.

Blumstein, Philip, and Pepper Schwartz. *American Couples*. New York: William Morrow and Company, 1983.

Dyer, Gwynne. *War*. New York: Crown Publishers, 1985.

Feuer, Lewis, ed. *Marx and Engels: Basic Writings on Politics and Philosophy*. Garden City, N.Y.: Anchor Books, 1959.

Fischer, Frank, and Carmen Sirianni, eds. *Critical Studies in Organization and Bureaucracy*. Philadelphia: Temple University Press, 1984.

Friedan, Betty. *The Feminine Mystique*. New York: W. W. Norton and Company, 1963.

———. *The Second Stage*. New York: Summit Books, 1981.

Herndon, James. *How to Survive in Your Native Land*. New York: Bantam Books, 1972.

Jackson, Philip. *Life in Classrooms*. New York: Holt, Rinehart and Winston, 1968.

Janis, Irving L. *Victims of Groupthink: A Psychological Study of Foreign-Policy Decisions and Fiascoes.* Boston: Houghton Mifflin Company, 1972.

Kagan, Jerome. *The Nature of the Child*. New York: Basic Books, 1984.

Keene, Karlyn, and Daniel Yankelovich. "American Values: Change and Stability." *Public Opinion* 6 (January 1984): 2–8; 21–35.

Kennan, George F. *The Nuclear Delusion: Soviet-American Relations in the Atomic Age.* New York: Pantheon Books, 1982.

Kohn, Alfie. *No Contest: The Case Against Competition.* Boston: Houghton Mifflin Company, 1986.

Lefebvre, Henri. *The Sociology of Marx.* Translated by Norbert Guterman. New York: Random House, 1968.

Levine, Adeline Gordon. *Love Canal: Science, Politics, and People.* Lexington, Mass.: Lexington Books, 1982.

Lockridge, Kenneth. *A New England Town: The First Hundred Years.* New York: W. W. Norton and Company, 1970.

Mannheim, Karl. *Ideology and Utopia.* New York: Harcourt, Brace & World, 1936.

Millett, Kate. *Sexual Politics.* Garden City, N.Y.: Doubleday and Company, 1970.

Schell, Jonathan. *The Fate of the Earth.* New York: Alfred A. Knopf, 1982.

Sizer, Theodore R. *Horace's Compromise: The Dilemma of the American High School.* Boston: Houghton Mifflin, 1984.

Sjoberg, Gideon, Ted S. Vaughan, and Norma Williams. "Bureaucracy as a Moral Issue." *Journal of Applied Behavioral Science* 20 (1984): 441–453.

Skolnick, Arlene, and Jerome H. Skolnick, eds. *Family in Transition.* 4th edition. Boston: Little, Brown and Company, 1983.

Slater, Philip. *Earthwalk.* New York: Bantam Books, 1975.

Weber, Max. *The Protestant Ethic and the Spirit of Capitalism.* Translated by Talcott Parsons. New York: Charles Scribner's Sons, 1948.

Whyte, William H., Jr. *The Organization Man.* New York: Simon and Schuster, 1956.

Williams, Robin, Jr. *American Society.* 3rd edition. New York: Alfred A. Knopf, 1970.

Yankelovich, Daniel. *New Rules: Searching for Self-Fulfillment in a World Turned Upside Down.* New York: Random House, 1981.

# Index

## About the Author

CHRISTOPHER BATES DOOB has been teaching sociology at Southern Connecticut State University since 1970. The second edition of his text, *Sociology: An Introduction*, will be published by Holt, Rinehart and Winston in 1988. His primary interests, both professionally and personally, are world peace, environmental health, and couple relations, all of which are important topics in this book.